12/84

To Dad
Merry Christmas
and a Joyous New Year

Much love,
Tracy

ROYAL
AIR FORCE

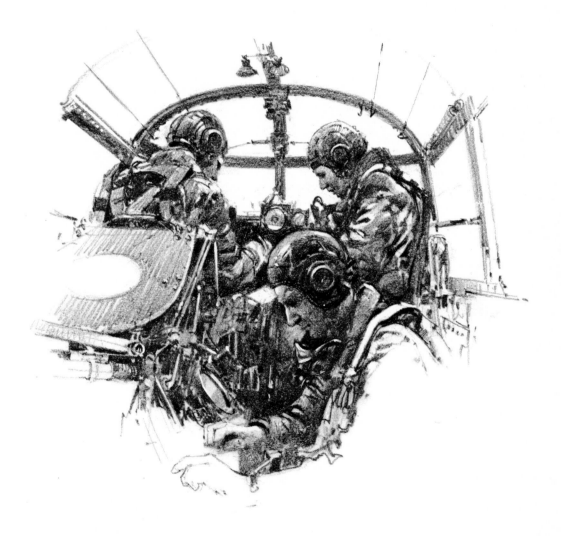

Lancaster aircrew

BAC Lightning interceptors

ROYAL AIR FORCE

The aircraft in service since 1918

Paintings by Michael Turner

Main text by Chaz Bowyer

Foreword by Raymond Baxter

Hamlyn

London·New York·Sydney·Toronto

To my late Parents, in appreciation of their unfailing support and encouragement.

© copyright Studio 88 1981
Second Impression 1982
ISBN 0 600 34933 0

Published by
The Hamlyn Publishing Group Limited
London · New York · Sydney · Toronto
Astronaut House, Feltham, Middlesex, England

Printed in Italy

Contents

Foreword by Michael Turner

As a small boy living in the suburbs of London throughout World War Two, I suppose it was not surprising that the exploits of the Royal Air Force in those heroic days captured my imagination, and filled me with an admiration which I have never lost. I still recall the endless nights under the dining-room table, sheltering from Hitler's bombs, and persuading my indulgent Mother to take me on hazardous journeys to airfields such as Northolt and Croydon, to peer furtively through any available gaps in the perimeter at Spitfires and Hurricanes being prepared for battle. This, coupled with my fascination with aircraft and flying, which developed over the same period, has no doubt led me to what is largely a labour of love.

In attempting to portray and record the aircraft of the RAF in their many forms and spheres of operation over more than sixty years, I have, regrettably, had to omit many interesting types and incidents, and have had to try to epitomise the many aspects of some famous and extensively used types with but one interpretation; but, whilst only scratching the surface of my self-imposed task, I hope this collection, in itself a condensed selection from a more comprehensive series of paintings still evolving, will provide a worthwhile visual record, enhanced by an informative and interesting commentary by Chaz Bowyer as well as brief comments by many who flew the aircraft.

I believe strongly that, to be able to convey the true feeling and atmosphere of any subject, there is no substitute for personal experience, and I have gone to considerable lengths over recent years to acquire as many first-hand impressions as possible. In this respect, I have been fortunate enough to experience flight in various types of military aircraft – from Tiger Moth to Jaguar, Lancaster to Nimrod: from elementary flying in a University Air Squadron's Bulldog to team aerobatics with the Red Arrows. Of course, the majority of the aircraft in this book are beyond the scope of my personal involvement, being as they are from times past, but, nevertheless, the feel of flying in an open cockpit, wire-braced biplane, the gut-wrenching *G*-forces encountered in a modern high-performance jet, the wearing of often cumbersome and uncomfortable flying clothing and the nauseous smell of an oxygen mask, give one an understanding which imparts a sympathy that can be applied to the situation one is trying to portray.

As I have said, most of the aircraft in this book are beyond the range of my personal experience; consequently, I have had to spend a considerable amount of time on research, and I have tried to ensure that the resultant paintings provide a reliable and historically accurate record of the subjects, colour schemes and settings depicted, if some anomalies have crept in, I offer my apologies.

I should like to record here my thanks to Chaz Bowyer for providing the commentary on each of the aircraft depicted. I should also like to thank the Ministry of Defence, and the various Squadron personnel who have assisted me so well in my quest for personal involvement over recent years, and must add that, in the process, I have acquired even more admiration for those skilled enough to be capable of controlling an aircraft under the extreme conditions of flight required by a military aircraft, and for those equally dedicated personnel on the ground who make such flying possible.

Michael Turner

Foreword by Raymond Baxter

The philosophical distinction between artist and craftsman has long been debated by those far better qualified than me, but that Michael Turner is both seems to me self-evident. Having known him and his work for more years than perhaps either of us would care to calculate, my regard for both remains undiminished.

To reproduce with such consistency so broad a diversity of highly technical subjects to the standards of blueprint accuracy demands the skill and studious devotion of the engineering draughtsman. Observe, for example, the rigging wires in his Avro Tutor (p. 56) or Walrus (p. 90), the aerials on his Demon (p. 57), or the relationship between skeleton and skin in his Handley Page Heyford (p. 48). This is the stuff to satisfy the most pedantic enthusiast for detail.

On the other hand, even without their primary subjects the background of so many of his paintings would constitute a work of art sufficient to satisfy more than one of his distinguished colleagues. The mountains below and above his Hawker Harts (p. 52) are awesome in their ice-clad majesty. Conversely the featureless monochrome behind his Vickers Vincent (p. 59) shimmer with mirages. Sky and desert merge in exactly the manner I recall as characteristic of certain days above Habbaniyah.

Sometimes perhaps, by purely aesthetic standards, his background is somewhat too cluttered. The famous Johnnie Johnson Spitfire painting is a case in point (p. 109). Turner has attacked the chaos on the airfield with the boyish zest for action of a ten-year-old.

Yet his restraint in, for example, the Knapsack power station leaves us in no doubt where we are – if only for a few pulse-racing seconds (pp. 84-85).

It is unusual in my experience to meet an artist so skilled in the detail of technology who yet enjoys an equal facility with the human figure. The 'erks' in the foreground of his 501 Squadron Vampires (p. 151) are sprawled on the grass precisely as 'erks' and grass become inseparable for any length of time when nothing more demanding was to be done. On the other hand one can smell the sweat of the toiling airmen at Kenley during the Battle of Britain (p. 76) and the posture of the trio and pair about the RE8 freezes all five figures in a micro-second of their activity (pp. 14-15). The men in the tender approaching the Sunderland stand as only boatmen stand in boats (pp. 92-93), and the weight and restriction of flying gear hampers the aircrew at 4 FTS Abu Sueir in 1938 (p. 56). Michael Turner was certainly never near Abu Sueir in 1938, but in this as in many other paintings of periods long before his time, he commands the authority of the eye-witness.

His choice and use of colour may be the key to his success in capturing the mood of the moment. Striking by any standards is the electrical storm through which his Hercules is lurching (p. 179), and the blue and white sky-scape pierced by his Lightnings is high-altitude, high-performance flying (p. 180). I can almost hear the hiss of the spray as his Blackburn Iris turns into wind (p. 39), and there is a dream-like quality appropriate to the Far East created by the greys and mauves of his formation of four Supermarine Southamptons (p. 32).

Some of his more 'experimental' skys – offsetting the SE5a's for example (p. 24), the

57 Squadron Lancasters (p. 104) or the Boulton Paul Defiant (p. 88) – are for me less successful. But the equally adventurous smudges surrounding his PR Spitfire 'high above the Mediterranean' (p. 135), and the stratified cirrus and shadow behind his inverted Meteors (p. 156), work the wonder of poise in limitless space.

To those worried by the 'chocolate box' image of graphic painting I would refer Michael Turner's drawings. His Gnat, with the crew strapping-in (p. 171); the Phantom (p. 181); the height of the Beverley embarking troops (p. 153); the 2nd TAF Mustang with its bomb in the foreground and church tower behind (p. 128) – all these are remarkable studies.

There remains one outstanding characteristic common to all his work. All his airborne aeroplanes are flying. Just how this is achieved I cannot say. It is a quality instantly apparent by its absence from the work of lesser aviation artists, and instantly recognisable to anyone who has flown.

Michael Turner is above all a pilots' artist.

Without a deep and undying love for flying and aeroplanes, none of his demonstrable skills as artist and craftsman could combine to achieve the evocative impact of his pictures.

The jacket photograph of Michael Turner speaks volumes. The smile framed by his 'bone-dome' is that of a man happy in his work. I know the feeling well, and that is why to anyone who shares it, his work commands the particular affection reserved to that of a fellow spirit with whom communication is in no way hampered by time or distance. The sounds, the smells, the feel of the controls, the squeeze of the *G* and the weightlessness of inversion – above all the quickening of the pulse – all come flooding back from every encapsulated moment of experience.

Aeroplanes come closer to being 'alive' than any other machines. In this collection Michael Turner has ensured the immortality of the aeroplanes of the Royal Air Force, and that is no inconsiderable contribution to bequeath to posterity.

Raymond Baxter

Briefing student pilots beside an Avro 504N

9

An SE5a in combat

Aircraft
of World War One

The advent of the war in 1914 diverted all aeronautical development into military aircraft. Designers produced two major types of reconnaissance aeroplane: the two-seat biplane with reasonable range and endurance, and, in much fewer numbers, small, single-seater, 'high speed' (*sic*) 'scouts'. Nevertheless, ideas for different tasks for aircraft were already being mooted, in particular for pure bomber and fighter designs; major examples of these being respectively the giant Handley Page 0/100 and the optimistically-titled Vickers 'Destroyer'. War Office and Admiralty orders were spread among a varied selection of private manufacturers throughout the war, resulting in a myriad of aircraft concepts ranging from excellent to frankly ridiculous. Even so, near-standardisation of aircraft types was relatively swift, and most were designed under one or other title–bombers, reconnaissance, scouts (to be later known as fighters), trainers, and various types of maritime floatplanes and flying boats.

From 1915 to 1918 the urgent exigencies of wartime quickened the development of each major type of aeroplane design for its succinct war role, and by April 1918, when the RAF was 'born', its firstline squadrons were well equipped in respect of specialised roles. Fighter units were flying Sopwith Camels, SE5a's, Sopwith Dolphins and the two-seater Bristol F2b; while day and night bomber squadrons were equipped with De Havilland 4 or 9 two-seaters, Handley Page 0/100 or 0/400 behemoths, and even the obsolescent FE2b or 2d two-seat 'pushers'. 'Artillery Observation' squadrons for direct tactical support of the army relied on the RE8 or Armstrong Whitworth FK8, and former RNAS units employed a variety of floatplanes or flying boats for maritime purposes. Even the UK-based instructional organisation was by then receiving aircraft specifically designed for training roles, while Home Defences had been allotted a number of squadrons equipped with crudely-modified fighters for night interception of German raiders.

Bristol Fighter

A rugged 'fighter-reconnaissance' design introduced to squadron operations in France from April 1917, the Bristol Fighter – known to its wartime crews as the 'Biff' and its post-1918 owners as the 'Brisfit' – quickly earned a fighting reputation which also led to its universally recognised title of 'King of Two-Seaters'. Strongly constructed, with excellent controls' response, manoeuvrability and overall performance, the Bristol F2b allowed its pilot to handle his machine like any normal single-seat fighter, with the advantage of a gunner to protect the tail; the latter adopting the age-old classic 'back-to-back' fighting stance with his 'driver'. Had the F2b rested on its many war-time laurels alone, it would have secured a niche in any list of classic aircraft designs; yet the aircraft was destined to continue in first-line service with RAF squadrons until early 1932. During those years, Brisfits gave sterling service on operations over Egypt, Palestine, Iraq and northern India (now Pakistan); they were virtually unaltered from their original concept, yet they successfully undertook almost every possible role.

Crew reactions to this aircraft were unanimous in their praises. The late Major W F J Harvey, MBE, DFC, TD, who fought in F2bs of 22 Squadron in 1918, said of it, 'This was a classic aeroplane in looks, in performance for its period, and of a curiously perfect tactical design at a time when the future requirements of a fighting aircraft were not fully understood . . .' Another 1918 pilot expressed his enthusiasm in equestrian terms, calling the F2b '. . . a thoroughbred hunter, with a delicate mouth and a stout heart.' Such was the appeal of the design that some 50 years later the test pilot Godfrey Auty, after piloting F2b D8096 of the Shuttleworth Collection, said of it, 'From the moment of placing one's left foot on the root of the lower port wing to hoist oneself into the cockpit, there is a feeling of unity between man and machine.'

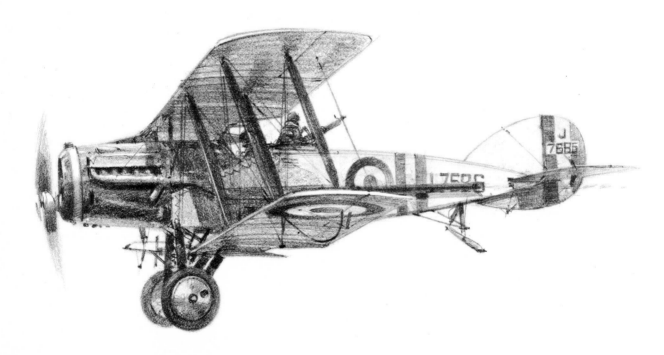

Captain E N Griffith, CBE, describes one of his experiences in the Bristol Fighter:

The Bristol Fighter was a magnificent, tough, stable flying machine with no hidden or design faults. I have tested it to the maximum, being caught, or 'jumped', early one morning on a single machine long-distance reconnaissance, thirty miles on the German side of the lines.

The chief objective was to locate and describe the end of the night railway activity from which the Intelligence Staff could calculate the movement of enemy troops, supplies and ammunition. We located the trains by the white smoke of the railway steam engines, since the great bulk of transport was then by rail not road. The Bristol Fighter would be about 15,000 to 18,000 feet up; a German single-

Bristol Fighter A Bristol F2b of 11 Squadron in combat with a patrol of Albatros DVs in poor weather. This aeroplane was as fast and manoeuvrable as many contemporary single-seater fighters, and was one of the most effective fighters of World War One.

seater fighter at least 1000 feet higher was in position waiting for the early plane each day. It was the cause of many losses and the mission was very dangerous and much disliked.

We took off before daylight, and on this occasion I was well over the enemy lines by 3 am. The Hun jumped me out of the sun, which at that time in July was on the north-eastern horizon. My job was to get back with my information, not to be foolish and

13

try to fight. The Hun dropped on me firing. I went down as vertically as possible with full engine on . . . turning to the right, then the left and doing every evasive action I could think of.

The Bristol Fighter was riddled by machine-gun bullets through the wings and the fuselage. The compass was just in front of my face – a bullet smashed into it, passing within an inch of my head, although, of course, I did not notice it at the time. The stay wires of the tailplane were also shot away.

My downward plunge with full engine on was kept up for 10,000 to 12,000 feet, I then adopted the 'falling leaf' stall manoeuvre that I believe succeeded in convincing the Hun that my observer and I were dead and the machine out of control until it crashed. He probably reported a victory, but I lived and got back to base, and had my most successful spell between then and September.

I recount this story to show that the Bristol Fighter was unbreakable. I did all I could at its maximum speed and it held together, beyond what was considered the speed at which it might break up.

Lieutenant Whipple was a young American who served in E N Griffith's Flight. In this account, written shortly after the event took place, he describes a dogfight between Bristol Fighters and the Richtofen Circus in August 1918:

My first fight was with a Hun two-seater who was directing his artillery fire from his side of the lines. All five of us dived on him firing as we went and if it had not been for his armour plate he would have been a sorry wreck. As it was, I was on the tail end of the formation and got last shot at him and saw him go wobbling down to the ground. All of us had shared equally in his ruin so no-one could claim official credit, but it put new confidence into me. I was sure my bullets had been effective and

RE8 The crew of an RE8 of 16 Squadron prepare to set off on a dawn patrol over enemy lines in 1918. In many ways, the RE8 resembled the BE2 which it began to replace from early 1917; by the end of hostilities the RE8 was in service with 19 squadrons and over 4000 were eventually manufactured.

MICHAEL TURNER

now I felt ready for anything at even odds. The chance came the very next day when we were escorting a flight of de Havillands to bomb a German rest camp. Day bombers require an escort of fighting machines for they cannot hold their own against agile fighting scouts. The bombers had finished their job and we were just starting for home when suddenly up from the east came fourteen Fokkers all painted a brilliant scarlet except the leader who flew a silver tri-plane. The bombers raced for the lines leaving the five of us to fight it out and cover their retreat. We did nothing but stick even closer together and wait for our flight commander to give a signal. The Huns were right up to us by now and started firing. Their method of attack was very peculiar. One by one they circled up to us, firing as they came. We paid no attention to them but kept on steadily climbing so that while they were losing height by so much fussing around we were gaining height. At last our commander Captain Griffith judged we had the height on them then, without a single warning of our intentions, we wheeled and dived on the whole fourteen.

My own gun jammed and would not fire, and there was no time to fix it. The German I had picked out for myself slipped away unscratched. I

was just pulling out of my dive when some instinct made me look over the side down to my right, just in time to see the big tri-plane getting into position to shoot me from underneath. My own gun was useless so I nudged frantically at my observer's elbow and pointed down at the Hun. He lost no time in turning his gun on him and the German changed his mind about attacking us and turned for home, but too late. Captain Griffith had seen my predicament and had come up to help me just in time to plunge after the fleeing leader of the German Circus. I turned to get a better view of the running flight. It did not last long. Inside of a few seconds the tri-plane was falling like a shooting star leaving a trail of smoke and flame a mile above it. We lost no time in getting home after this and when we landed and tallied up the score we found that we had shot down three of them and not one of our machines was seriously damaged. The next day we read in our secret intelligence files that 'On August 10 Lieut. Loewenhardt commanding the Richtofen circus was shot down by a flight of Bristol Fighters on the Somme front. Lieut. Loewenhardt had just achieved his 52nd victory'. Thus perished the crack German air fighter of that time. I could not help thinking how very near I came to being his 53rd victim.

RE8

Known universally as the 'Harry Tate' (one of the leading contemporary music-hall artists) the Farnborough-designed RE8 was one of the great workhorses of the RFC and RAF during the latter years of World War One. Its intended role was reconnaissance in aid of the infantry, a task which included photographing enemy-held territory behind the trenches, low-level contact patrols with forward units of the Allied armies, and constant assistance to the artillery on spotting patrols for the heavy guns. Plodding in performance and sluggish in manoeuvrability, the RE8 was no real match for the sleek Fokkers and Albatros Scouts of 1917-18, and its crews suffered high casualty rates. Yet one of the commonest sights of the aerial war in 1918 was of lone RE8s doggedly flying monotonous

figures-of-eight paths through a flurry of anti-aircraft shell-bursts, as their courageous crews maintained faith with the earthbound infantry they were supporting.

Standardised for army co-operation duties by 1917, the RE8 was nevertheless by no means ideal for war operations. With its longitudinal *and* lateral in-built dihedral it became known as the 'Riggers' Nightmare', while its all-round mediocrity in performance meant that its many solid achievements in daily routine tasks were a tribute to the fortitude and sheer courage of its crews, rather than any credit to the aircraft or its designers. That it continued in frontline service until the end of hostilities was a mark of the irresponsibility and ignorance of RAF higher authorities of the day.

De Havilland 4

Prior to its operational debut with 55 Squadron RFC in early 1917, the DH4 was rumoured to be a war-winner with a speed, ceiling, and range of action which would give its crews virtual immunity from anti-aircraft fire and opposing fighter assaults. In practice this two-seat day bomber did not live up to its reputation initially, but by 1918, with modification and a more powerful engine, it became recognised as probably the finest day bomber in the Allied air services. Though its two-men crew were located in cockpits too far apart for ideal crew co-operation, the DH4's outstanding qualities in performance and range outweighed any minor disadvantages, and its basic design was to be perpetuated for many years after the war in a wide variety of civil and military roles, both in Europe and especially in the USA; in the latter case providing the backbone of the emergent air mail services.

In service the DH4 proved to be reliable, sturdy and a near-ideal platform for accurate daylight bombing operations. As such it was employed widely by the British air services and, during the closing months of the war, by the US air bombing units. Its war ceiling in excess of 20,000 feet kept it out of normal anti-aircraft fire zones, while its diving speed to lower altitudes on return often outwitted pursuing enemy fighters. Nevertheless, the pilot's forward location placed him in the unenviable position of being seated between the engine and the main petrol tank. In the event of a crash-landing, he faced a choice of being crushed by the engine or cremated by any ensuing fire; a situation which contributed to the DH4's initial soubriquet of the 'Flaming Coffin'.

Squadron Leader C P O Bartlett, DSC:

On June 3, 1917, I came up against my first enemy fighter and he proved to be as stout a foe as any I encountered. Four of us, Le Mesurier, Gardener, Dickson and myself, left at 4.00 am on DH4s for Burges docks, a strong wind taking us to our target by 4.30 am. We were met by very heavy and accurate AA fire. The other three dropped their bombs and turned for home, but my gunlayer, Sambrook, signalled a second run. Every battery was now concentrated on us and, slideslip as I would, I could not shake them off and thought every next salvo must get us. Several times the old DH4 was tossed bodily by their blast. At last after what seemed an eternity, a moment, I comforted myself that they had got tired of wasting ammunition on us.

My complacency was short-lived, violent signals from Sambrook indicating danger from below and, banking steeply, I saw a small, vicious fighter hurtling up at us at great speed. On his first dive he got a burst through my dashboard, shattering much of it on the port side, another bullet went through the feed of one of my Vickers guns, the other already being jammed.

With tracers passing all round and through us, I could also see our tracers passing all round and

De Havilland 4 DH4s from 27 Squadron bomb enemy lines in the battle for Amiens in March 1918. This light bomber could carry 460 lb of bombs and had a top speed of over 130 mph.

apparently through the V-strutter Albatros. He nevertheless dived on us three times, closing to point-blank range on each dive, and I could see his head clearly as he turned away. One or other of us *must, I felt, go down within the next minute or two. At last, after his third dive, to my intense relief, he dived away steeply, but apparently under control.*

Sambrook had let that V-strutter have three full trays and it was a miracle we did not get him – or he us!

Handley Page 0/400

The HP 0/400 was a giant of an aeroplane in every way. With a wing span of 100 feet, length of nearly 63 feet, and height of 22 feet, it overshadowed every other operational aircraft of the RAF in 1918. Derived from a 1914 design, the 0/400 first entered service as the 0/100 bomber with 3 Wing RNAS in 1916 and continued in service as a long-range night bomber until the end of the war; some 400 examples being delivered ultimately to the services. Its massive wings were designed for folding back to ease ground handling and field accommoda-

Handley Page 0/400 Two Handley Page 0/400s from 215 Squadron bomb the Badische Anilin Chemical Works at Mannheim on the night of 25 August 1918. The two aircraft attacked at a very low level (250 and 500 feet).

tion, and it carried a normal bomb load of 14 or 16 bombs of 112 lb. It was the only aircraft to drop the largest, heaviest Allied bomb of the war, the 1600/1650lb SN (some 40 of these giant missiles being dropped in the closing months of the struggle). Post-1918 use of the 0/400 was mainly confined to the emerging passenger and freight carriage airlines; the last RAF examples were replaced in service by 1922.

In the current era of supersonic aerial transport it may seem quaint to recall the first impressions of flying in an HP 0/400 by a national newspaper reporter in September 1918, 'The roar of the two engines becomes a perfect inferno as we start to climb. The pressure of wind on my face makes me wonder if it will yet behead me. On each side of me a brown line of exhaust gases flows from the motors. The gale of wind thrust past my head by the whirling screws is so tremendous that it seems as though I was being forced through something solid like butter . . .' All this at a speed of little more than 60 mph! First of the true heavy bombers of the RAF, vehicle for the genesis of strategic night bombing, and faithful pioneer of the first peacetime airlines in Britain; the HP 0/400 holds a unique position in British aviation annals.

Leslie Blacking was 19 years old when as a Second Lieutenant he flew 0/400s on 27 Squadron at Ligescourt near Abbeville:

I remember this big bomber chiefly for the heaviness of its controls and the height of its cockpit above the ground. It had to be flown all the time and it was particularly heavy on lateral control. When you put on bank it didn't respond at once. When it did you had to reverse the joystick wheel immediately to take the bank off, and if you went over 45° you were in trouble. I've actually had to stand up to exert all my strength to get the 'bus' back on an even keel.

The 'Handleys' were used for night bombing attacks on strategic targets, such as railway marshalling yards, and ammunition and fuel dumps, to help stem the German offensive of 1918. I had done only ten hours flying on 0/400s before joining the squadron and had previously flown the tricycle-undercarriage FE 2bs; consequently I found it difficult to judge my height before touch-down. The observer helped my landing problem by leaning over the side and yelling, 'Back, back, more—OK!' As we always switched-off the engines and glided in I could hear him quite clearly, and knew when to pull back on the control column wheel to get the tail down.

Our grass airfield wasn't very big, but it had a wide valley on two sides, where the River Authie ran, and this helped us to get our heavily-laden planes into the air.

The instrument panel was quite simple: compass, airspeed indicator, bubble, altimeter and clock. There was a larger compass on the floor beside the pilot who sat on the right. The counters were

outside the cockpit—on the engine nacelles.

We had no armour-plating or parachutes, just fabric and wood around us and thin duck-boarding under our feet. Our greatest fear was fire in the air, if we were to be hit by any of the green 'flaming onions' or white phosphorous balls which arched up through the darkness from the ground defences.

Normally we carried a number of 112 lb bombs but sometimes just one 1650 lb bomb, and when we let it go the 0/400 rose about 50 feet.

We could stay airborne for about 4½ hours—if you could stand the cold; for it was intense, despite our heavy flying gear (which could be electrically heated), in that big, open cockpit.

Sopwith Camel

Ask anyone to name just three aircraft of the 1914-18 aerial war and the answer is certain to include a pug-nosed, waspish little killer called the Camel. This 'popping firecracker' emerged from the war as the most successful individual fighter used by any nation, its many pilots claiming almost 3000 combat victories. Its aerobatic qualities were legendary. It could be flick-rolled at grass-cutting height without loss of altitude and looped from a low speed with complete confidence. Yet its most significant characteristic was an ability to turn left or right and reverse flight path under perfect control with the speed of a greased pond-skater. Thoroughly unstable and wilfully independent, the Camel offered little sympathy to any ham-fisted tyro, but those who mastered her found themselves equipped with probably the greatest dogfighter of the war.

Veteran Camel pilots were unanimous in their praises of the Camel. Major W G Moore, OBE, DSC, said of it, 'A skilled pilot could not wish for a better mount. To him it was like having a pair of wings strapped onto his shoulder blades'; while Henry Woollett, a 36-victory ace, gave his opinion that, 'The Camel could dictate a fight and turn inside any scout the enemy used, if it was operating at the right altitude, usually around 12,000 feet.' Major Oliver Stewart, MC, AFC, summed most pilots' regard for the type succinctly, 'Gifted with a more strongly developed personality than perhaps any other aeroplane, the Sopwith Camel inspired pilots who flew it with respect and with affection . . . it set a new standard in powers of manoeuvre and even today (*1936*) it probably remains the most highly manoeuvrable aero-plane that has ever been built.' Such were the quicksilver qualities of the Camel that the fears of student pilots and the praise of combat veterans are best described by the blunt phrase of one veteran when he said of the 'fierce little beast', 'She left you with three choices: Red Cross, Victoria Cross . . . or wooden cross . . .'

Cecil Lewis, MC describes one of the first night operations:

After being wounded and returning from France in the summer of 1917, I was posted to Hainault Farm, a Home Defence aerodrome just beyond Ilford. It was there I met the Sopwith Camel, so called because of a slightly 'humped' top line to the fuselage. The pilot was hunched in behind the flat engine, the tanks were the full depth of the fuselage just behind the pilot—and all this meant the weight was highly concentrated and made for very lively handling characteristics. The Camel, in fact, was a beauty. It was sturdy enough to stand rough flying in a dogfight, handy enough to outmanoeuvre anything it came across. In addition it had two Vickers guns firing through the propellor and soon proved itself a very offensive weapon indeed. Beyond all this, it had all the Sopwith characteristics of viceless, well-balanced handling. It was light, responsive, comfortable and pilots loved it.

The forward stagger of the main planes gave the pilot a good forward and downward view which served him well in a dogfight; but later, when the machine began to be used as a night fighter, to attack enemy bombers at home or overseas, the positions of pilot and tank were reversed. This brought the pilot out just aft of the main planes and gave him an excellent forward and upward view. Although we did not think the Camel handled

quite as well with this arrangement, it was better suited to the job.

When I joined the squadron at Hainault, the defence of London wasn't a very serious affair. There had been one or two isolated daylight raids; but these had been at long intervals. But suddenly one September evening, we had news about dusk of a flight of German aeroplanes approaching the Thames Estuary, and in half an hour the whole character of Home Defence changed.

It is difficult for anyone today to understand such a situation. In 1917 night flying was unheard of. Apart from one or two heroes who went chasing Zeppelins in BEs, nobody dreamed of going up at night. I had done several hundred hours in the air, but I had never flown at night. There was no night

Sopwith Camel Sopwith Camels from 65 Squadron attack an enemy observation balloon near the Flanders front in September 1918. This single-seater fighter was named 'the Camel' because the top line of the fuselage was slightly 'humped' to accom- modate the breeches of its twin Vickers guns.

training. No cockpits were fitted with any instrument lighting. No dials were luminous. We were caught completely unawares.

It was just luck I happened to be in the Mess. Most of the chaps had already left for town. With one or two others we quickly togged up and got the machines out. We raided the stores for hand torches and climbed on board. We ran up the engines and checked the revs and oil pressure with the torch, *flipped it off and put it back into our pockets—all the rest would have to be luck and airmanship.*

Somebody rigged up a line of flares, paraffin-soaked cotton waste burning in a bucket. A typical smoky smell always to be associated in my mind with that first night flight. I taxied along the flare path, turned into wind, and with that mixture of trust and stoicism all pilots know, pushed open the throttle.

A second later I was reassured. Magically, lyrically reassured. For the dreaded blackness was a wonderful misty landscape in which the Thames Estuary, like a pool of silver, bisected the Kent and Essex coasts, every roof top reflected the radiance of the rising moon, the plume of smoke from an approaching train lay like an ostrich feather on the woods. An exquisite, silent fairy-like world of mist and meadow was spread below me. No need to use the torch! I could hear my engine revs, feel my air speed and I knew my country.

So I continued on up to 14,000 feet, watching the probing searchlight beams, looking for Archie bursts to help me to locate the enemy and noting a few heavy red glows lower down from the heart of London where the bombs were bursting. Never on that occasion, or on dozens of other patrols during the next six months did I see a sign of the enemy. One or two lucky men, like 'Flossie' Brand (one of our flight commanders) ran into Gothas and promptly shot them down. (Flossie went in so close that he singed his eyebrows when the Hun caught fire). But generally our patrols were two-hour stretches of frustration, for although it appeared one could see for miles, the moving speck of an aircraft

anything more than 100 yards away was invisible. All we could hope to do was locate the glow of an exhaust. Home Defence was a pretty slow business.

Reassuring on that first night were the golden pinpoints of the burning flares—like brooches of light on the dark earth. Soon we could find our way all around the area by the pattern of these flares. That night I came down rather fast, anxious about the landing, determined not to stall short of the field. The air was clear down to 10 feet, then, suddenly, I was in a thick white blanket of mist. The flares came up through it, bursting on me as I passed them. It was eerie and anxious, but quickly came the reaction 'I must be almost on the deck'. I cut the engine, held her off and a moment later the wheels rumbled. All was well!

Back in France a year later the golden brooch of flares had gone because the German night bombers found it an attractive target for their eggs. We were forced to use a trolley about six feet long fitted with three Aldis lamps. On returning to the airfield, the pilot gave his call sign by flashing the recognition light on the belly of the aircraft, the trolley turned on the lights, the aircraft landed in their beam and the lights went off immediately.

It wasn't much to land by and France without flares was quite easy to get lost in. The new flashing beacons that should have served to give us our bearings were new and strange. So one of my pilots, quite lost, his petrol running low at the end of a two-hour patrol, was delighted to see the beams of the Aldis landing trolley below him. He came down, undershot, went round again and landed—on a road, in the beam of car headlights, 150 miles from home!

SE5a

Of the many aeroplanes designed at the Royal Aircraft Factory at Farnborough before and, especially, throughout 1914-18, very few were received with enthusiasm by the crews who had to fly them in combat. One of the rare exceptions was the SE5a. The result of several years of progressive development, the first SE5s were taken to France by 56 Squadron in April 1917. Combat experience quickly led to much modi-

fication and improvement in engine power, and the resulting SE5a came to be regarded as probably the finest wartime product from Farnborough. Though having a tendency to nose-heaviness in ground handling, in the air the SE5a had no vices. It was immensely strong in construction, permitting high speed dives with confidence, had positive control responses in almost any attitude, and withstood the

inevitable rough handling associated with close dogfighting without undue stress on the airframe. Its relatively high speed, excellent ceiling performance, and all-round robustness made it a near-ideal vehicle for the 1917-18 mode of air fighting, and it became the mount of a high proportion of the many top-scoring fighter pilots of the Allied air services.

The SE5a's huge contribution to ultimate aerial supremacy over the Western Front particularly may be gauged by the opinions of two men who flew the type. Oliver Stewart said of the design, 'It is of all aeroplanes the richest in the associations of aerial fighting, of hard-contested and long drawn-out "dogfights", of battles against heavy odds, of extraordinary

SE5a A pair of SE5a's from 56 Squadron on dawn patrol near Valheureux, France. Typically the aircraft was fitted with one Vickers gun firing through the propeller and one Lewis gun mounted on the upper plane to fire over the propeller.

escapes.' Cecil Lewis, who led the first SE squadron to France, said of it, 'The SE5 was probably the first fighting aircraft to be produced which was reliable enough and steady enough to stand up to the rough and tumble of 30 or 40 aircraft milling around trying to shoot each other down . . . Slammed into a dive, yanked into a climb, pulled hard round in a very tight turn, the aircraft structure had to stand up to enormous and sudden strains. The SE came through this ordeal triumphantly and justified the belief of the top brass that it would give the Allies the supremacy of the air that year. It did.'

J V Gascoyne, DFC has described how the SE was used in the closing months of the war for groundstraffing:

It was the practice to take off singly, carrying four Cooper bombs and fully loaded with ammunition. I found it most exciting to fly over the enemy trenches and batteries, sometimes at a height less than 200 feet. This was not as dangerous as it appears for we were moving very fast (for those days) and so were difficult to hit, particularly as we were firing our own guns most of the time. The danger came from crossfire and field guns using shrapnel. On the top centre-section of the SE, a Lewis gun was carried with a drum containing 97 rounds. To reload this gun one had to pull it down on a slide into the cock-pit. The pilot was given a certain amount of protection by a small wind-screen, measuring 11½ inches by 3 inches. To fit a new drum was therefore a work of art and very *few pilots attempted it. It was not only very difficult but it took quite a time and left you open to attack by an enemy machine. We had no bomb sights but it was astonishing how near one could get to the target after a little practice and experience. My own plan was to decide on a target while flying at low-level and so gain experience as to how far the bomb carried. One had to be careful, however, with the bomb moving forward at the same speed as the aircraft as you both arrived at the target at the same time if the pilot flew in a straight line. It was therefore necessary to turn away from the target before the bomb arrived.*

Felixstowe Flying Boat

Once man-controlled flight had been accomplished it was perhaps inevitable that Britain, with her age-old maritime traditions, should adapt the aeroplane for sea-going roles. The most outstanding examples of a true maritime design were the various large flying boats produced during 1914-18, collectively known as the Felixstowe or F-boats. Directly derived from the ideas of the noted American avaiator Glenn H Curtiss, the F-boats were designed by John C Porte, a British naval officer serving in the RNAS. Porte's unceasing efforts to provide the RNAS with bigger and better flying boats continued until his death in 1919, and his legacy to Britain was the long line of practical designs which formed the foundation for several decades of RAF flying boat design.

Intended mainly for patrolling coastal waters, to protect Britain's mercantile lifelines of imported goods and materials, the F-boat crews were never content to play a mere watch-and-ward role, and took every opportunity to get to grips with any enemy which came within fighting range. At least two Zeppelins were destroyed in air combat by F-boats, while the many pure dogfights between British flying boats and German seaplanes during 1917-18 epitomised the offensive spirit of all F-boat crews. F-boats were big by any standards, with wings spanning 100 feet or more in several cases, weighing in excess of 10,000 lb fully loaded, and capable of patrols of six hours or more.

Professor Sir Austin Robinson, CMG, OBE, FBA flew Felixstowe Flyingboats in the

RNAS and RAF before beginning a distinguished career as an economist:

At the time they were built, the F2As were the largest operational aircraft apart from the Handley Page 0/400. They were beautiful aeroplanes, although with hindsight their defects can be seen. For example, although the F2A had a rather short tail, rudder and fin, it had very long wings which meant that the ailerons were further from the centre of gravity than the rudder was; the obvious consequence was that if you tried to pick up a wing, you found yourself swinging off your compass course. However, one learnt by experience to give the rudder a hefty kick while using the ailerons, and on that basis a fairly accurate compass course could be maintained. The F2A also had difficulty in taking off in a heavy swell when fully loaded, although it could take off in less than fifteen seconds when lightly loaded in calm conditions.

The functions of the F2As differed at each station. Felixstowe and Yarmouth frequently encountered German seaplanes, because they were battling to keep control of the air in the lower North Sea. Throughout the war important trade took place with the Netherlands, which was neutral, and frequent convoys we knew as the 'beef trips' had to be defended by them from German attacks. At Killingholme, we seldom encountered German seaplanes; instead we had two main tasks. First, we undertook anti-submarine patrols, which were usually fairly close in-shore. Secondly, we undertook fleet reconnaissance and intercepted and frightened off Zeppelins.

Zeppelins had a higher ceiling than the F2A, and so we could only hope to catch one unawares or, more often, scare it away by making it drop its ballast and fuel in gaining altitude to avoid us and return home. The only Zeppelin that Killingholme has been given credit for was the L62, which was shot down by Pattinson, although others believe that this to be doubtful.

Felixstowe Flying Boat An F2A May Harden May flying boat spots an enemy U-boat while on an anti-submarine patrol in 1918. In action the second pilot would operate the two guns in the nose, the engineer the gun next to the pilot, and the radio operator fired through a porthole.

A Supermarine Stranraer flying boat

Aircraft Between the Wars

By the Armistice of November 1918 a number of promising new aircraft were in embryo for the RAF, but as peacetime demobilisation and severely reduced financial backing decimated RAF strength, Britain's new air arm was forced to compromise in all matters of equipment, and the few remaining squadrons in 1920 relied on wartime-designed machines such as the Bristol F2b, DH9A, Vickers Vimy and Sopwith Snipe. In the event, the F2b and DH9A were to soldier on in frontline operational use until the 1930s.

Continuing this policy of compromise through the 1920s, the RAF contracted aircraft manufacturers to produce a series of 'General Purpose' designs – a broad description indicative of the multi-varied roles each was expected to undertake – resulting in such aircraft as the Westland Wapiti, Vickers Vincent, and a line of Fairey III variants. On the bomber-cum-transport scene were lumbering biplanes like the Virginia, Vernon, Valentia and Hyderabad – all little better in performance or conception than their 1918 predecessors. In the fighter-interceptor role, for defence of Britain, the RAF continued to rely on twin-gunned biplanes until well into the 1930s, equipping firstline squadrons successively with Grebes, Gamecocks, Bulldogs, Furies, Gauntlets and Gladiators – neat, highly manoeuvrable little aircraft which were delightful to fly but increasingly obsolescent in design concept for the more modern requirements of an aerial arm.

De Havilland 9a

The DH9a, or 'Ninak' as it was more familiarly known to its crews, shared with the Bristol F2b fighter the brunt of the RAF's firstline operational duties throughout the 1920s. Entering squadron service in the closing months of 1918, the Ninak was then chosen as the main day bomber to equip many of the much-reduced RAF's overseas units attempting to maintain air control of Britain's empire and mandated territories; particularly in the Middle East zones and in India. A development of the much-criticised DH9 of 1917, the Ninak showed a significant improvement in engine power and consequent high altitude performance over its predecessor. In the heated thin air of Iraq or India, however, the Ninak's all-round performance suffered badly offering a fast landing

De Havilland 9a A flight of DH9a's on patrol against dissident tribesmen in Mesopotamia (now Iraq) in 1926. The DH9 was an 'improvement' on the DH4, but in fact was inferior because of its less powerful engine – the 9a (the 'Nine-Ack' or 'Ninak') had the more powerful Liberty engine.

speed but a laborious rate of climb. Despite inadequate maintenance facilities and financial backing almost throughout its 'peacetime' years, the DH9a and its stoic crews undertook a wide variety of operational roles successfully.

While India and Iraq saw the biggest concentration of Ninak operational employment, the aircraft did useful work in many other areas. In Africa a handful helped pioneer the vogue for long distance proving flights; while in Britain from 1925, DH9a's formed the initial equipment of several squadrons of the freshly-created Auxiliary Air Force. Like all old soldiers the Ninak faded away from RAF service and by 1932 few were in evidence. Essentially a military aeroplane – hardworking, dependable – and displaying real fortitude when called upon to operate in conditions above and beyond the call of duty; the DH9a was a stalwart of the RAF's adolescence, and will always be remembered with affection by those who flew and maintained them.

Supermarine Southampton

The immediate post-1918 years saw the tiny RAF's coastal protection units equipped mainly with wartime-designed flying boats and other seaplanes, and it was not until 1925 that a postwar design of flying boat began to re-equip the squadrons. This was the Supermarine Southampton, designed by R J Mitchell who later was to 'father' the Spitfire prototype. The Southampton was to set a pattern for future RAF flying boats and served for some ten years in firstline use – hence its nickname 'Old Faithful' by its crews. Early versions of the Southampton had wooden-constructed hulls, but these were eventually replaced by metal-hulled Mark II versions which eliminated the natural impediment of some 400 lb added weight of sea-water soakage in the wooden-hulled types. Southampton crews pioneered many of the long range cruises of the late 1920s, testing endurance and in-flight maintenance, and virtually fostered the self-dependent

character thereafter associated with all RAF flying boat crews.

The most publicised exploit by Southampton crews began in October 1927 when four aircraft of the Far East Flight set out from Britain and eventually completed some 24,000 miles of flying to Singapore, Australia and around the China Sea without serious mishap – an event heralded in the contemporary press as 'the greatest flight in history'. Various attempts to modify and extend the life of the Southampton were modestly successful, but after nearly ten years of faithful service the Southampton was finally retired from the RAF – a longevity all the more remarkable when it is realised that an all-Mark production of the type only amounted to 78 aircraft.

G E Livock, who was one of the pilots on the Far East Flight, has written about some of the problems they encountered *en route*:

31

The selection of refuelling places took a great deal of working out on account of the limited range of the aircraft—about 500 sea miles was a safe maximum in still air. On a few occasions we had to make do with very unsatisfactory mooring sites. It was well known that most of the danger to flying boats occurs when they are on the water. They are then vulnerable not only to bad weather, but also to attacks by sight-seeing motor boats, drifting native river craft and, of course, refuelling boats.

We each carried a hand-pump to pump the petrol up to the tanks from a sump built into the centre section. The petrol boat was secured to the moorings and held alongside while the tins or drums were lifted up and the contents poured into the sump. We never knew what sorts of craft would

Supermarine Southampton Supermarine Southamptons of the Far East Flight, which became 205 Squadron, after their epic 27,000-mile cruise to India, Australia, Hong Kong and Singapore.

bring out the petrol, and we sampled Chinese sampans, primitive native boats, motor boats, dinghies and large barges. Their crews seemed to think that a flying boat was built like a battleship and that they could come alongside at full speed. The whole flying boat crew would turn out to repel boarders and exercise their vocabularly of expletives. Occasional damage was done, but we became very expert at fending off these assaults.

Our first real test came on the leg from Alexandretta in Syria across the desert to Baghdad, a distance of 480 sea miles. Owing to a strong downdraught, we had difficulty, with our full petrol load, in climbing over the cloud-covered mountains. Once over the desert we were met by an increasing headwind with alternating dust and rain storms, which reduced visibility in place to a few hundred yards. After more than eight hours in the air we ran into a thunderstorm and, as it was clear that we did not have enough fuel to reach Baghdad, we landed on the River Euphrates at Ramadi and anchored for the night. There was a store of petrol at the local RAF emergency landing ground and we took thirty gallons for each boat, which we brought off in our rubber dinghies. The night was made miserable by thunderstorms, howling jackals on the banks and the boats swinging wildly as first the 5-knot current and then the 20-knot wind took charge.

We stayed for three weeks at Karachi to enable the base party to carry out a thorough inspection of the aircraft, which were hauled up on to a beach. After Karachi we were not to see another RAF station until we landed at Hong Kong a year later.

In some ways the flight down the west coast of India to Ceylon was the most interesting and certainly the most entertaining of the whole cruise. As far as I know, no aircraft had ever flown that way before and, as news of our programme had been sent ahead, the inhabitants of whole districts flocked down to the beaches to watch us pass. It was an extraordinary sight to see miles of beautiful sandy beach crowded with thousands of Indians, all looking up as we flew over their heads.

Armstrong Whitworth Siskin

Although it was not until May 1924 that the first Siskin III fighters entered RAF service – with 41 Squadron at Northolt – the origin of this stubby, angular little fighter stretch back to 1918 at Farnborough when the Siddeley-Deasey SR2 Siskin was first constructed. The following years saw a lengthy progressive development of the SR2 basic design until its emergence as the RAF's Siskin III and IIIa fighters. The Siskin III was, in fact, the first all-metal frame aeroplane to be built in quantity for the RAF, and the design formed an interim link in progression from the wartime concept of fighter aircraft to the peacetime heavier and all-metal constructed interceptors of the 1920s and 1930s. The Siskin also pioneered the use of short-wave radio telephony in fighters of the RAF.

Armstrong Whitworth Siskin Siskin IIIa's from B Flight, 32 Squadron, practise aerobatics over the English countryside in 1929. The Siskin was one of the first fighters to be ordered in quantity by the RAF after the end of the war.

Despite its rather ungainly looks, the Siskin is perhaps best remembered for its many aerobatic exhibitions, particularly 43 Squadron's formation drills with aircraft linked together by elastic cords.

Oliver Stewart, who test-flew the Siskin at Martlesham Heath, has recorded his impressions:
It was an awkward-looking machine – a great, uncouth brute of a thing, but with a heart of gold.

Extremely easy to fly, the Siskin was gentle, easy-going, calm, good-tempered . . . amenable to discipline and would do loops, rolls – both flick and slow – and spins graciously, if not very quickly. The outlook was markedly good and the cockpit arrangements and flying qualities comfortable. The Siskin was above all things a comfortable machine – a human machine, and it ministered to the comfort and convenience of its pilot in more ways than one . . . it was certainly an exceedingly safe machine.

Fairey III

With successive variations and modifications, the Fairey III series of land- and floatplanes served in the RAF and the air services of several other countries. Originating from two 1917 experimental Fairey designs, the first Fairey IIIAs saw brief service in 1918 and were steadily improved until the first IIID appeared in August 1920. Simply constructed, tough and reliable, the IIID was extraordinarily versatile and may be regarded as Fairey's most successful aircraft in general terms. Convertible from landplane to floatplane configuration easily, the IIID saw extensive use with the RAF and the Fleet Air Arm in many guises, and is particularly remembered for its many long distance proving flights in the Middle East and African zones; pioneering routes which were later to become standard flightpaths for Imperial Airways and its successors.

One pilot who flew IIIDs described them as 'Large, heavy and clumsy', and went on to say, 'It had been designed as a seaplane and, naturally enough, it made a better seaplane than a landplane. It carried two passengers in addition to the pilot, had a maximum speed of about 120 mph, and an endurance of four and a half hours. The Napier Lion engine gave very little trouble except for cooling system water leaks, and in four years' flying from Leuchars we only had one forced landing directly due to engine failure, and that could have and should have been avoided. The IIID was the despair of pilots who liked to do 'pretty' landings, for it had a gliding angle rather like that of a brick, and then "fell out of your hand" without any warning. However, it was so strongly built that it was difficult to damage it.'

The pilot G E Livock has given the following account of using the Fairey IIID on reconnaissance in Malaya in the mid-1920s:

Each morning the duty seaplane was wheeled out of the hangar and prepared for take-off. One of the cranes on each side of the hangar doors was swung inwards, and the patent slip hooked on to the wire slings on top of the centre section of the fuselage. If the weather conditions appeared favourable the order was given to hoist out. The engine was started and the pilot and observer climbed on board. After testing his engine, the pilot indicated that he was ready, and the RAF duty officer, standing on deck with a small flag in each hand, signalled to the crane driver for the plane to be hoisted a few feet off its trolley. The crane was then swung outboard until the aircraft was clear of the ship's side. When the signal was given, the seaplane was slowly lowered until the floats were just touching the water. The duty officer then signalled 'slip' to the observer, who was standing on top of the fuselage. The observer jerked the quick release. The seaplane dropped gently into the water and taxied away for take-off. In two or three minutes the aircraft was in the air and climbing towards the area chosen for the

Fairey III Fairey IIID floatplanes of 202 Squadron fly over Marsaxlokk Bay, Malta in 1929. Over 200 IIIDs were manufactured and they were widely deployed; this included service with the carriers *Argus* and *Vindictive* (in the inter-war period the RAF operated the Fleet Air Arm).

day's photographs. About half an hour later, at ten thousand feet, the observer began to give instructions to the pilot.

Communication between pilot and observer was by rubber speaking-tubes; earphones were sewn into the flaps of the 'solar bowlers' which we wore instead of flying caps. The solar bowler was a half-sized topee and was supplied because it was, quite erroneously, considered almost certain death to go out in the mid-day sun without thick protection on the head. The observer, peering through the bottom of the cockpit, told the pilot which way to turn until the aircraft approached the starting point and was on the right course. The starting and finishing points of each strip were chosen so as to be easily identifiable from the air, for example, a railway station, a prominent headland or a river mouth.

A minute or so before passing over the starting point the observer said: 'Steady as you go. Starting camera in one minute'. The pilot concentrated hard on maintaining his height at exactly ten thousand feet, and adjusted the trim of the aircraft so that it kept absolutely level and on a steady course. During the run along the strip the observer gave the pilot any

minor alterations to his direction, and kept an eye on the camera to see that it was working properly. It was not easy flying, for we had none of the delicate instruments one has today, but just the standard sluggish old 'clocks'. However, we had plenty of practice and eventually became very expert. After completing two or three strips our time was up: we would then have been in the air for one and a half to two hours. The throttle was eased gently back and we began the long slow glide towards the ship.

It was necessary to come down very slowly to prevent condensation forming in the camera and film boxes due to the great variation in temperature. It was wonderfully cool at ten thousand feet and one was quite happy to be wearing a flying-coat and scarf. For the first few thousand feet of the descent there was only a slight rise in temperature, but at about two or three thousand feet the hot pungent smell of the jungle suddenly enveloped the aircraft. Off came the scarf and the flying-coat was unbuttoned and opened wide. By the time one flattened out to land the heat seemed intolerable, and prickly heat, which had been dormant in the cold, burst out again.

Blackburn Iris

After two years in the making, the first Iris was launched in June 1926 with a wooden hull, but the following year was converted to the Iris Mk II by having its superstructure refitted to a new metal hull. Only eight other examples were built thereafter, but one of these (S1593) was eventually redesigned as the prototype RB3a Perth – the ultimate Iris development and the largest biplane flying boat ever used by the RAF. Of sound design and extremely strong construction, the Iris came to be used for a number of very long range flights around the world, and various modifications were made progressively both to improve the basic design and to increase crew self-sufficiency, including the provision of an 80 lb five-man duralumin dinghy carried inverted on the lower centre section. Remaining in service until the early 1930s, the various versions of the Iris were subjected to a bewildering variety of technical

improvements, many of these on a testing basis for future flying boat requirements. In particular, S1593, titled *Zephyrus*, which was delivered to 209 Squadron in July 1931, had its bow compartment enlarged to accommodate a 37 mm Coventry Ordnance Works (COW) cannon – an unwieldy form of armament which quickly became dubbed the 'Flying Battleship' in the popular press of the period.

Often referred to as the Iris Mk VI, the Blackburn Perth development differed externally from its 'parent' design by having enclosed pilots' cockpits. Only four examples were constructed and these stayed in RAF service until 1936 before being relegated to experimental use. The success of the Iris, Blackburn's first venture into flying boat design, led to construction in 1930 of the Blackburn Sydney, which was a high-wing monoplane flying boat. Its hull was patently derived from the Iris, and

though the Sydney was never awarded a production order, it was the first British military monoplane flying boat of the heavy-weight type.

Wing Commander F L Petch flew on all 245 sorties of the Blackburn Iris S1263:

His Majesty's Flying Boat, 'Iris' Mark III, Service No S1263 was built by the Blackburn Aircraft Company Limited at Brough, East Yorkshire in 1929. She was the first production model from the design of Major Rennie and was destined for service with 209 (Flying Boat) Squadron which reformed at Mount Batten, Plymouth in January 1930.

The Iris was designed as a long range, ocean-going aircraft to augment the coastal patrol

Blackburn Iris A Blackburn Iris Mark III flying boat of 209 Squadron taxis out from Calshot, Hampshire for an evening return-flight to its base at RAF Mount Batten, Plymouth. This was one of the largest of contemporary aircraft – its wingspan was 97 feet.

services so ably fulfilled hitherto by the squadrons of Supermarine Southamptons. She was powered by three Rolls-Royce Condor engines, each of 675 hp.

Only the one squadron was equipped with Iris aircraft, first with the Mark III which later, by modification, became the Mark V and ultimately with what might well have been a later mark, but was, in fact, designated the 'Perth'.

The armament of the Iris consisted of Lewis guns in bow and midship positions with a third one at the tail end of the hull which, however, had only limited arc of fire. In the bow position, a one-pounder gun, made by the Coventry Ordnance Works, and consequently known as the 'Cow' gun, could be mounted, and indeed was, once every year for demonstration purposes, thus providing the press with an annual opportunity in publish pictures of 'Britain's Aerial Battleship'.

S1263 was launched on 5 February 1930 and, after a trip only five minutes short of five hours, completed her maiden flight to her home base at Mount Batten. From that day, for her life of nearly three years with 209 Squadron, she performed those duties for which she was built, without any claim to fame, with few dramatic highlights and rarely achieving press mention beyond her own parish, until her last day's duty. Her total contribution to the defence of the shores of Britain could be statistically presented as 245 sorties, totalling 343 hours in the air. Unimpressive perhaps almost laughable, by modern criteria, but some will remember that fifty years ago flying intensities were, of necessity, much lower and the business of maintaining serviceability not always

the simple task today's engineers might believe.

An early summer spent in home waters and air provided what was perhaps the most pleasant of existences available to the Royal Air Force, with one heart-fluttering exception. 209 Squadron, ever eager to help others, was acting as target aircraft for the Siskin fighters of 1 Squadron.

The Iris had a blind spot right under the tail, because the tail gunner could not depress his Lewis gun sufficiently to keep a fighter in his sight. The mid-ships gunner had to wait patiently for the Siskin pilot to stall turn under the tail after the attack, hoping that he might be careless enough to go wide of the tailplane tips, when he could get him (with a camera of course).

On this bright spring morning, S1263's engineer was in the midship position. He watched the fighter coming up under the tail, saw him making his turn; knew that he would go wide and was waiting for the kill when, instead, in his sights, he saw one of the four intertailplane struts come adrift at the top and fall down. The horror of that moment was literally speechless, for in those days there was no intercom. There was a hurried securing of the camera gun and a scamper through the hull with two minutes in an atmosphere of 'What the hell is this chap on about?' before the captain truly appraised the situation.

Then followed possibly the most gentle turn and the longest glide since Kittyhawk, until S1263 slid gratefully down on to the surface of the English Channel. Twenty minutes later it became known that three out of four fittings were defective. Thus are modifications conceived.

Hawker Horsley

Intended initially to be a medium day bomber, but later more remembered as a land-based torpedo-bomber, the Horsley first entered RAF squadron use with 11 Sqn at Netheravon in January 1927. It remained in service for eleven years, and two Horsley units, Nos 36 and 100 Squadrons, were despatched to Singapore as the first land-based RAF torpedo units to serve overseas. May 1927 saw the first of three

attempts to fly a modified Horsley non-stop from Cranwell to India. None achieved their goal, though the first flight at least briefly created a new world long distance record.

One RAF pilot who knew the Horsley well, the late Tommy Lucke, has recorded his memories of the aircraft:

Two versions were built – day bomber and

Hawker Horsley A Hawker Horsley from 100 Squadron drops a practice torpedo during a sortie from Donibristle, Scotland in 1931.

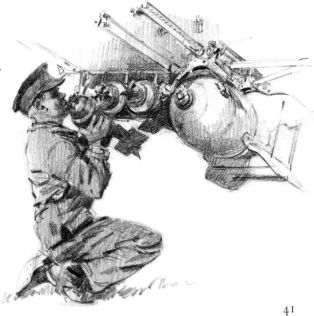

torpedo-bomber, and neither was a thing of beauty. It was without vice except on the ground. With its very wide chassis and no brakes, it was difficult to taxi downwind, even with the aid of aileron drag . . . taxying downwind across a slope could be impossible. Although the aircraft would loop, stall turn, and spin in the most gentlemanly manner, it could not be said to be fully aerobatic. In a straight stall the Horsley was extremely stable and, with the stick held hard back, could be kept quite level at a negligible forward speed and what appeared to be a very low rate of descent. During dive-bombing practice the ring and bead sights, and hence the whole aircraft, were lined up on the target by the pilot. As communication with the bomb-aimer via Gosport Tube was inadequate, a string was run from the control column to the bomb aimer's right ankle. At what he judged to be the appropriate moment, the pilot yanked the string, and the bomb-aimer immediately yanked the manual bomb release toggle. With practice this Heath Robinson approach to an exact science turned out to be surprisingly accurate.

Bristol Bulldog

The Bulldog represented the most successful of the earliest attempts by British manufacturers to produce a fast-climbing, fully aerobatic, interceptor fighter, and the prototype first flew in May 1927. Service examples first reached 3 Squadron in May 1929, and within three years nine other squadrons were equipped with Bulldogs; thereby representing some two-thirds of the UK's contemporary home defences. Regarded by all pilots who flew them as probably the best aerobatic machines of the day, Bulldogs featured largely in the annual air displays at Hendon; performing highly accurate formation flying, trailing coloured smoke and undertaking superb individual aerobatics. Bulldogs remained in RAF squadron use until 1937, though several two-seat variants were still flying two years later at 4 FTS, Egypt. The only Bulldogs to actually see war operations were 17 machines sold to Finland in early 1935, which saw brief action during the Winter War of 1939.

Frank Tredrey's impressions of his first flight in

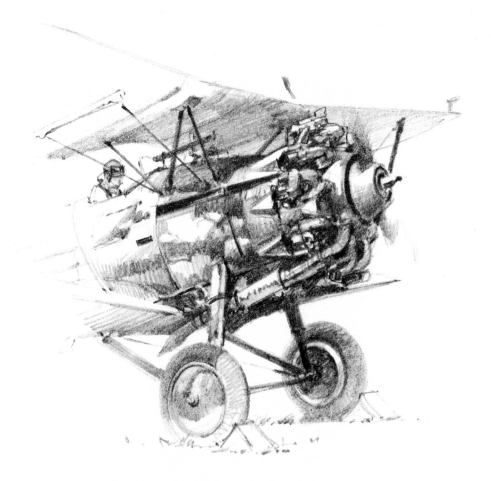

a Bulldog reflect the esoteric delight experienced by most pilots of those pre-1939 days of RAF flying:

Four of them were being warmed up by the fitters as we walked over, line abreast heading into wind, their fat short little bodies hugging the ground, their thick and stubby airscrews making the dust fly as they tore around and pulled the wheels against the chocks. Green and silver backs and yellow wheel-shields, air-screw spinners and cowling gun channels. Cockpits fairly crowded with instruments and levers and direction plates . . . In the Bulldog you half lie back. The straps are tight over your shoulders, your legs straddled out to reach the rudder bar, your right fist on the spade grip and your left closed round the big throttle lever. You

Bristol Bulldog Bristol Bulldogs from 19 Squadron in formation at the 1934 Hendon Air Display, led by Flight Lieutenant Harry Broadhurst. This aircraft, which was the RAF's standard fighter in the early 1930s, had an immensely strong steel frame that enabled the aircraft to withstand a great deal of stress; other advantages included a forward-placed cockpit that gave the pilot a good field of vision and easy changing of fuel tanks in the upper wing.

taxi out bumping and rocking vilely, your toes ready to stab on the footbrakes if she won't stop swinging in the wind. After (Avro) Tutors she fairly leaps off the ground, and climbs at a rate of knots. In level flight the airspeed needle sticks around the 130 mark, well throttled back to cruising revs.

Avro 504N

The 1918 Avro 504K trainer received a virtual new lease of Service life in 1927 when the last major variant of that doyen of RAF instructional aircraft was re-engined with a Lynx radial and fitted with a new form of undercarriage. The resulting 504N remained in production until 1933, and thereafter, on being sold off to a variety of civil companies, was responsible for giving many thousands of people their baptism of the air on joy-rides. Within the RAF it helped to pioneer instrument flying instruction ('blind flying') from late 1931; and gave splendid service in the RAF, AAF, and overseas at 4 FTS, Abu Sueir, Egypt. Though eventually replaced by its stable-mate the Avro Tutor, by 1934, seven civil 504Ns were recalled for duty with the RAF in 1940, to form a Special Duty Flight at Christchurch.

Allen Wheeler, who flew Avro 504Ns at Henlow in 1927-28, recalled:

Like its predecessor, the Lynx Avro, as it came to be called, was quite impressive in aerobatics, being able to do almost everything that other aeroplanes could do, and indeed one manoeuvre which most other aeroplanes could not do; this manoeuvre we called the Bunt. It involved pushing the aeroplane over into a dive and then further over until it was flying level but inverted . . . It was possible to trim the Avro 504N in a glide, with the engine just above idling power, and it should land itself without the pilot doing anything. The landing was, of course, a bit untidy but safe enough: one could taxi in after it anyhow. They were excellent for recreational flying of all kinds—even visiting friends in the neighbourhood, since they could be landed in any reasonable field and left idling for a long time.

Avro 504N An Avro 504N from Cambridge University Air Squadron flies over Stonehenge. This was the last of innumerable variants of the 504, and was also known as the Lynx Avro after its Lynx radial engine.

44

Hawker Fury

The sleek Hawker Fury I, which first equipped 43 Squadron at Tangmere in mid-1931, gave the RAF its first fighter in squadron service able to exceed 200 mph with a full warload. Highly aerobatic, the Fury was also at least 30 mph faster than any existing RAF fighter; while its performance and control response was summed by one ex-25 Squadron pilot as '. . . perfectly delightful'. Epitomising the elegant Fury's manoeuvrability and instant response were the four Furies of No. 1 Squadron's aerobatic team, which gave many superlative exhibitions of formation flying at the annual Hendon Displays of the late 1930s. Fury Is eventually equipped just three squadrons – Nos 1, 25 and 43 – but remained in frontline use until the outbreak of World War Two. In 1932, however, the manufacturer began development of the original design, resulting in the Fury II (illustrated)

Hawker Fury Hawker Fury IIs from 27 Squadron taxi forward ready for take-off. The Fury was faster than larger contemporary fighters and had an excellent rate of climb. It was an ideal single-seater interceptor.

which first flew in December 1936, and entered unit service with 25 Squadron in the same month. Within a year four more squadrons received Fury IIs, and nearly 100 examples were built, but their Service life was brief, being gradually replaced by 1938. With its uprated Kestrel engine, and spatted wheels, the Fury II showed a 20% increase in speed, and 34% improvement in rate of climb over its predecessor.

Handley Page Heyford

The Heyford will always be remembered primarily as the last biplane heavy bomber to enter RAF squadron service – the ultimate 'cloth bomber'. The first prototype made its first test flight in June 1930, and commenced its Service life with 99 Squadron at, appropriately, Upper Heyford in late 1933; one of the new designs to assist the early stages of RAF expansion from its 1920s' doldrums. Its distinctive configuration included such novel features as the 'shoulder' upper wing attachment to the long slender fuselage, the much-lowered bottom wing in which a thickened centre-section accommodated its bomb load, and the ventral 'dustbin' gun cupola for under-tail defence. Eleven squadrons were eventually equipped with Heyfords, and although replacement designs began to arrive in these units from 1937, Heyfords still lingered on several units until late 1939, and the Heyford was not officially declared as obsolete until mid-1941.

Heyford pilots generally liked the huge biplane; it was sturdy, agile – more than one Heyford was actually looped without mishap – while the ground crews found the aeroplane relatively simple to maintain and arm. In February 1935 one Heyford (K6902) was the RAE test vehicle for radar experiments, and

Handley Page Heyford Handley Page
Heyford bombers of B Flight, 10 Squadron,
on a training flight during the summer of 1936.

later that year air-tested the first airborne
radar transmitter conceived by Dr Robert
Watson-Watt and his colleagues. The last
'active' Heyford was still airworthy at Carding-
ton as late as August 1944; but the most vivid
memory of the 'Jolly Green Giant' for most
contemporary people was the immaculate
formations of Heyfords which flew at pre-1939
Hendon Displays, and especially the Royal
Review of the RAF by HM King George V in
July 1935 at Mildenhall and Duxford.

Boulton Paul Overstrand

Ponderous, slab-sided, angular in outline, the Overstrand was never a thing of beauty, while its Service use was restricted to merely equipping one squadron. Nevertheless, the Overstrand has an important niche in RAF history as the first RAF bomber to be fitted with a power-operated, totally enclosed gun turret, mounted in the nose. This unique fitment is perpetuated still by the squadron badge motif of a turreted tower by the only Overstrand unit, 101 Squadron. Other refinements novel for its period included an enclosed pilot's cockpit, cockpit heating, and a large protective windscreen for the mid-upper gunner's position, automatic pilot, and Townend rings for the two Pegasus engines.

The sheer strength of the Overstrand and its fluid manoeuvrability were convincingly demonstrated at Hendon in June 1936. Sgt

Boulton Paul Overstrand A Boulton Paul Overstrand of 101 Squadron under simulated attack from a Hawker Fury of 25 Squadron during gunnery practice in 1937. The plane's power-operated, enclosed gun turret can be seen clearly.

Reddick of 101 Squadron was 'attacked' by three Furies of 1 Squadron, and put his bomber into a series of half-rolls and superbly-executed loops which '. . . stopped simultaneously the breath of 200,000 people below'. Still harassed by one Fury, Reddick next pulled the bomber up on its tail, stalled, flicked its nose past the vertical, eased out of the dive and then resumed his original flightpath, leaving the Fury baffled. With a top speed of more than 150 mph, the Overstrand could give most contemporary fighters a run for their money, and the design was popular with its air and ground crews, offering few serious problems despite its bulk and varied innovations imposed by its designers.

Westland Wapiti

The Wapiti was in effect a compromise between official desire for a replacement for the ageing DH9a and Bristol F2b equipping most overseas squadrons of the RAF, and the need for strict economy in the contemporary parsimonious annual budgets for the RAF. From seven other contenders for an official contract, the Wapiti found favour because of its utilisation of certain DH9a components and spares readily available in the RAF's 'larder' at that time. The first units to receive Wapitis were squadrons in Iraq in 1928-30, while the first Wapiti squadrons to arrive in India were Nos 11 and 39 in October 1928. By early 1932 all eight India-based squadrons were operating the type. In all-round comfort and performance the Wapiti was a great improvement on its predecessors, and for the next ten years the Wapiti bore the brunt of operations among the mountains and hills of India's North-West Frontier (now Pakistan). Moreover, Wapitis formed the equipment of the first Indian Air Force unit when this service was inaugurated in April 1933; while in Britain Wapitis were flown extensively by several AAF squadrons.

From a pure flying viewpoint pilots found the Wapiti to be strong and thoroughly stable, responding easily to controls and, if required, fully aerobatic. One of the design's few vices was a permanent tendency to swing strongly on take-off and, especially, landing, thereby requiring 'Stick right back and fully stalled if you wanted a neat three-pointer' – a characteristic which, in view of the lack of brakes, often led

to 'expensive' landings. The Wapiti remained on active service in India until 1940 with the RAF, but continued in squadron use with the Indian Air Force for a further two years before being phased out.

Westland Wapiti A Wapiti of 30 Squadron sets off on patrol over Iraq in 1932, on policing duties for the League of Nations. The Wapiti was a two-seater 'general purpose' aircraft, and could be fitted with wheels, floats or skis.

Hawker Hart

Graceful and elegant in appearance, the Hart was also efficient. On equipping 33 Squadron in January 1930 it promptly outpaced every contemporary RAF fighter. Yet the Hart's greatest claim to fame was its extreme versatility and adaptability, being the 'father' to a long and prodigious variety of Hart derivatives in subsequent years. In September 1939 the RAF still held more than 1600 Harts and variants on charge overall—a sixth of the service's grand total of aircraft. Even after war was declared Harts continued active opera-

Hawker Hart Hawker Harts from 11 Squadron in flight over the Himalayas during a patrol along India's North-West Frontier. This two-seater single-bay biplane bomber was so successful a design that it gave rise to a long line of derivatives (including the Hawker Demon discussed on page 56).

tional duties in India until 1942, while the many Harts relegated to training roles during the 1930s virtually trained the bulk of Bomber Command's crews of the early war years.

Group Captain Frank Tredrey recorded his first flights in a Hart in his delightful book *Pilot's Summer* as follows:

She has a tendency to swing to the left as you

take off, which has to be firmly counteracted with right rudder; and you can see a frightful lot of ground ahead over the tapered nose when you're in flying position . . . climb seems rather steep after Tutors because she's much more powerful . . . straight and level flight, once more you can see a lot of ground ahead, and until you've watched the altimeter for a time and noticed that it doesn't register a change, could swear that you're diving her . . . turns very nice, with a Hart you can rip into a turn and out again as smoothly as slipping down a water-shoot . . . spinning, nice and slow. Needs full

opposite rudder to make her come out. Aerobatics? Far easier than Avro 504N, Tutor or Atlas. Plenty of loading in rolls off a loop . . . Landings a little bit tricky. On a windy day you have to get the stick back that last little bit in double quick time or else she drops on to a nice springy undercarriage and goes up like a lift to about five feet, half bouncing and half ballooning with the wind under the wings . . . give her a touch of throttle as she sinks she'll stay down all right the second time . . . I gave her a good fat burst and she sat down like a two-year-old.

Vickers Virginia

Although the Vimy of 1917 was Vickers' first successful venture into heavy bomber design, the Virginia of 1922 *et seq* is usually regarded as the real 'father' to the line of large Vickers biplane bombers and transports which were to give some 20 years service to the RAF. Built on strictly utilitarian, lines, the 'Ginnie' served its masters well, seeing RAF service mainly from 1924 until 1937, with a few examples even soldiering on in minor capacities until as late as 1941. It was progressively modified and developed throughout its long life, and provided an embryo bomber force's crews with their basic experience. Its ultra-steadiness on bombing runs is exemplified by the Ginnies of 7 Squadron which captured the annual Lawrence Minot Trophy for bombing no less than eight times against all opposition. Its regular appearances at each RAF Display from 1925 to 1937 made it a particular favourite with the public; while its years of acting as a platform for parachute training of air and ground crews will be well recalled by hundreds of ex-RAF men.

In view of its outstanding Service longevity it is perhaps surprising to note that, fully loaded, a Virginia could seldom exceed 100 mph in flight; while its nominal 3000 lb bomb load and ever-open crew cockpits were direct throwbacks to 1914-18 vintage designs. Notwithstanding its ancient charisma, the Virginia was beloved by its four-man crews; a dependable, rugged packhorse which seldom failed them.

Group Captain Sawyer flew Vickers Virginias in 1934 and remembers them with affection:

I had graduated from Cranwell in 1933 and joined 7 Squadron which flew Virginias. To a keen young airman of those days it was something of a joke. It looked like a great big flying bird-cage in which were a crew of four: pilot, second pilot who also navigated, wireless operator who also worked the front gun and a rear gunner. The Virginia was very easy to fly, but fully loaded it could only trundle along at 80 mph, which was slower than many First World War aircraft.

The Virginia also resembled First World War aircraft in that it had an open cockpit, or rather three as the rear gunner operated a Lewis gun mounted at the back in what was known as the 'dustbin' and the wireless operator had to crawl forward to another front open cockpit to use the front Lewis gun. The rear gunner could not get up to the main cockpit, but simply climbed into the dustbin and stayed there throughout the flight. His only method of communication to the pilot was the speaking tube, or 'Gosport tube'.

The Virginia was very steady on bombing runs, but its slow speed could mean that air currents greatly affected it and this particularly affected the rear gunner. I remember that one fine summer's day I moved into the dustbin on a photographic trip. Sitting there, I realised that even very gentle manoeuvres by the pilot would yaw the tail around horribly, and that the slightest movements caused by air currents would be greatly exaggerated for the

Vickers Virginia Among its other roles, the Virginia was used for parachute training in the mid-1930s by which date it was reaching the end of its operational life as a bomber. For this purpose parachute jump-off platforms were fitted behind the wing-tip struts as is shown in the painting.

rear gunner. I don't know how they endured it.

These comments may seem highly critical of the Virginia. In fact I and most of my contemporaries felt of lot of affection for the aeroplane, but by this time it had been in service for over a decade, and it did seem terribly old-fashioned.

Avro Tutor

By the late 1920s the RAF's need for a modern replacement for its ageing Avro 504 training aeroplanes resulted in the Avro firm producing a new, two-seat biplane with welded steel structure, the Avro 621, initially merely titled Trainer but soon relabelled as Tutor. Under the latter name the type was adopted by the RAF in June 1932 as the Service's standard *ab initio* instructional machine, which it remained until 1939 with nearly 800 Tutors being built and delivered. Its non-corroding superstructure, albeit fabric-covered, made the Tutor suitable for use in most climates, and the type became a familiar sight not only in Britain but also at the RAF's chief training school, 4 FTS at Abu Sueir, Egypt. Usually doped in a bright yellow colouring – a warning to all other aircraft that its occupants were almost certainly student pilots – Tutors were highly aerobatic; a facet superbly exploited by some of the Central Flying School instructors of the 1930s, whose inverted formation aerobatics in Tutors were a highlight of the Hendon Displays.

One pilot's initial reaction to flying his first Tutor was succinct, 'Gentlemanly little things from the flying point of view. Nicely balanced controls, light and smooth to handle, beautiful for all manoeuvres, no tricks or vices, sweet glide at seventy, and as easy to land as buttoning up your coat. Neat instrument board, excellent hidden and yet easily accessible

arrangement of controls, hand-lever wheel brakes, and the usual slots.' The present generation may still witness the neat flying always associated with Tutors by virtue of the sole airworthy example existing in Britain, K3215, at present owned and regularly exhibited by the Shuttleworth Collection at Old Warden aerodrome in Bedfordshire.

Avro Tutor An Avro Tutor stands ready, as student pilots prepare for a day's flying at 4 Flying Training School, Abu Sueir, Egypt in 1938.

Hawker Demon

On its introduction the speedy Hart bomber was able to outstrip all contemporary fighters with such ease that Hawkers immediately set about designing a fighter version – in Sydney

Camm's reported phrasing, 'Let's set a Hart to catch a Hart.' Modifying the first production Hart J9933, the new two-seat variant was initially titled the Hart Fighter, but soon after

Hawker Demon A Hawker Demon from 600 (City of London) Squadron practises dive-bombing off the Chesil Bank during summer camp in August 1938. The Demon was a variant of the Hawker Hart bomber (see page 51), and was the first two-seater fighter to be ordered by the RAF since World War One.

was renamed Demon. In this guise it revived the 1918 concept of a two-seat fighter – the first such for the RAF since that war. In view of the Demon's top speed of nearly 200 mph, however, serious thought was given to protection of the rear gunner from the effects of slipstream, and commencing with J9933 a number of Demons were fitted with a Frazer-Nash 'lobsterback' folding metal cupola over the rear cockpit. This armadillo type of screen hardly solved the problems of hand-wielding a Lewis gun in high speed combat, but at least afforded a degree of pure physical comfort to the wretched gunner.

The first Demon squadrons began receiving their aircraft in 1933-34, but in September 1938 when the Munich crisis erupted seven of Fighter Command's full strength of 28 squadrons (including the AAF units) were still flying Demons. Had war with Germany resulted at that time it is difficult to imagine how their crews would have fared against the Luftwaffe's latest fighters. By the following September no Demons remained in squadron frontline service, though almost 140 were still on RAF charge in various locations. At least 64 Demons were delivered to Australia, the first batch of 18 forming the new equipment of 1 Squadron RAAF, though these were used for army co-operation and bombing roles in addition to their intended fighter task.

Vickers Vincent

The Vincent was merely one of several little-publicised, hardworking aeroplanes used operationally by the RAF. A direct variant of its stablemate the Vildebeest torpedo-bomber, the Vincent carried an extended range fuel tank between its undercarriage legs, plus all the military paraphernalia commonly associated with army co-operation aircraft of the period serving in overseas commands. Joining its first squadron in late 1934, the Vincent equipped 11 squadrons in all – each unit being based in the Middle East zones. An ungainly design, with few concessions to streamlining or other aerodynamic refinements, the Vincent proved very reliable and enormously tough while operating in conditions of extreme heat and primitive landing grounds. They were still in frontline squadron use when the World War Two began, and saw plentiful action in East Africa during 1940-41 and in Iraq in 1941. In the context of pure progression in engineering techniques, it might be noted that the Vincent was Vickers' last design constructed by the traditional metal-frame, tubular fuselage et al. After the Vincent the firm turned to using the geodetic airframe construction patterns conceived by the eminent inventor and designer Barnes Wallis.

Philip Middlehurst flew as a passenger in one of the last operational Vincents:

After two years based in the UK and 78 Squadron, Bomber Command, I had been posted to Aden, and found myself in charge of a group of Arab-manned radio outstations scattered around the mountains and deserts of the protectorate, and which provided communications for the Government Colonial Administration Service. In most cases flying by Vincent was the only convenient way to reach them.

Starting up the Vincent was quite a lark. It entailed climbing up on to the lower mainplane, reaching out, full extent, and opening a drop-down flap just ahead of the pilot. Then one had to do a sort of sideways splits movement and step on to the flap with one foot. Once there, a starting crank had to be unclipped from inside the hole revealed by the flap and fitted into the inertia starter gear. At temperatures which were often sizzling at about 110°F it was hot work, to say the least, to crank away until the required revs were reached (judged by the starter's whine). All this had to be done right-handed whilst the left hand reached out to engage the dog-clutch lever, and at the same time one shouted 'Contact' to the pilot. If all this sounds like a one-man-band in action, it must have looked even funnier to anyone who witnessed it.

If the engine did cough into life, which rarely happened at the first attempt, the really hairy part began for the 'startee'. About two feet from where you were standing on your insignificant foothold was that enormous brute of a prop. With the pilot blipping the throttle to clear the engine, one had to

replace the starting handle, foot-fumble for the wing, assisted by the blast from the propeller, and, once there, turn to shut the flap and screw home the quick-release studs. From there on it was only a matter of weaving between the flying wires and diving headfirst into the middle cockpit.

Vincent crews must ever have been a spartan breed. Ventilation in the open cockpit was no problem but seating, apart from the pilot's substantial throne, was primitive. The wireless operator had a swivel seat, and the canvas-laced steel-tube-framed fuselage hardly came higher than his elbows. When the aircraft bounced and jinked around through the turbulence over the mountains the clip-on canvas safety belt which snapped on to his parachute harness was the greatest of comforts.

Vickers Vincent A Vickers Vincent from 55 Squadron circles over the Iraq Command Boat Club sheds at Habbaniya, its home base in 1938. This three-seater 'general purpose' aircraft served throughout the Middle East and Africa until 1942 and saw action against the Italians in East Africa.

In the centre cockpit the seat was even more spartan. It was a plain board which was suspended from steel cables at each corner, and as the Aden 'flying kit' usually consisted of a helmet, shorts and a battle-dress tunic, the seat made its impression quite soon. In its bombing role the Vincent had been equipped with a sliding hatch from which the bomb aimer, lying prone in the tunnel, could aim his deadly wares. There was only one snag to this

59

arrangement. The hatches would never stay shut and were quickly forced wide open by the slipstream. Still, familiarity breeds contempt, they say, and one got quite used to perching suspended by the swaying cables and watching the brown earth rolling by perhaps 12,000 feet down between your bare knees.

The gap left by the demise of the Vincents was never adequately filled. Their replacements, Fairey Albacores, might have looked vaguely similar and could take off and land in the same tight corners, but they were no match when it came to carrying awkwardly shaped freight. Then again, after all that fresh-air flying in the old Vincents they were just that wee bit on the civilized side.

Vickers Valentia

In 1920, when the Vickers firm was already engaged in planning what was to become their Virginia bomber, the firm was also asked to tender for the design of a troop-carrying military transport aircraft. The first outcome was a design later called the Victoria, and this initiated a family tree of developed variants which gave birth to the Valentia. This was in essence a more powerfully engined Victoria with wheel brakes and a tail wheel to replace the tail skids on its predecessors. Additional strengthening of the structure meant greater weight-carrying capability. Entering squadron service in May 1934, Valentias operated in most overseas theatres and accumulated an impressive number of flying hours over deserts and mountains in Iraq, Egypt, and India. Patient, plodding workhorses, the Valentias carried troops or freight over the barren wastelands with steady regularity.

The outbreak of war in 1939 merely accentuated the importance of air transportation, particularly in the overseas theatres of war, and the outdated Valentias continued to give trojan service in the Middle East, but especially in India, where 31 Squadron's Valentias continued to operate until well into 1942. Even as late as 1943 a few examples were still in use as pure communications 'hacks'; while the last-known Valentia to survive, K3600, was sold to the Indian government in July 1944. The Valentia, with its forebears the Victoria and Vernon, founded what was eventually to blossom into RAF Transport Command, and in addition were instrumental in pioneering many of the overseas civil air routes around the Far East.

Vickers Valentia A Vickers Valentia military transport of 31 Squadron, which in 1938 was engaged in troop-carrying operations in India.

61

Handley Page Harrow and Fairey Hendon

The urgent need for expansion of the RAF set into motion in the early 1930s coincided with a period in British aircraft design when emphasis on the monoplane configuration was mounting. In 1935 the Air Ministry ordered 100 Handley Page Harrows as troop carriers but by early 1937, when the first Harrow reached its squadron, the design had become a bomber. Within that year five squadrons became Harrow-equipped. Of simple yet impressive outline the Harrows served as 'interim' heavy bombers until 1939, when most reverted to their original intended role as transport vehicles. In the latter role Harrow Transports – usually nicknamed 'Sparrows' – provided sterling service in several war theatres.

Another monoplane bomber, of much earlier conception, was the Fairey Hendon. Built to the same 1927 specification as the biplane Heyford bomber, the Hendon was literally ahead of its time. Procrastination by the Air Ministry meant that this successful 1927 project was not actually awarded a contract until 1934, despite the Hendon's obvious superiority over its biplane contemporaries. In the event the Hendon – the RAF's first all-metal constructed, low-wing, cantilever monoplane heavy bomber – did not enter squadron service until November 1936, and then only fully equipped one unit, 38 Squadron, based at Mildenhall and, later, Marham. Capable of carrying some 2500 lb of bombs on internally accommodated racks, enclosed by automatic doors, and with wings spanning just over 100 feet, the Hendon presaged a much later generation of heavy bombers. Only 14 Hendons were built, and the final 11 were withdrawn in July 1939.

Handley Page Harrow and Fairey Hendon
A 115 Squadron Handley Page Harrow runs up its engines prior to a flight from Marham, Norfolk, while a Fairey Hendon from 38 Squadron passes overhead.

Mechanics load a Short Stirling

Aircraft
of World War Two

The hasty resurgence in rearmament from the mid-1930s brought with it a flood of fresh designs from which emerged the age of the metal monoplanes, replacing the canvas-skinned biplanes of long and faithful service. Twin-engined monoplane bombers such as the Hampden, the Blenheim, the Whitley and the Wellington began to reach RAF squadrons in the late 1930s, while open-cockpit Gauntlets and Furies began to be replaced by eight gun Hurricanes and Spitfires. More significantly, a decision was taken to equip a future Bomber Command with a fresh generation of four-engined, strategic, heavy bombers, ultimately exemplified by the Stirling, the Halifax and the Lancaster. When war came in 1939, however, the RAF was still at a transitionary stage of modernisation, with all Commands still equipped with a mixture of biplanes and monoplanes. It was to remain so for at least two years of war before finally gathering sufficient strength of strike power to begin a true air offensive against Germany. In the interim several new aircraft came into service – most significant of which was the radical all-wood constructed DH Mosquito bomber which in subsequent years was to be seen in most operational forms. Even as such new designs reached squadron service the jet-engined aeroplane was being secretly developed. The first examples in RAF service were Gloster Meteors in 1944 – harbingers of a new era in RAF aircraft.

Vickers Wellesley

If for no other reason, the Wellesley has a particular niche in RAF history for being the first aeroplane to introduce the unique Barnes Wallis geodetic, or 'basket-weave', style of construction to operational service. Its active service record, however, added honours to the Wellesley and its crews. The first production aircraft were delivered to the RAF from March 1937 to 76 Squadron, the first unit to be fully equipped with the type. Eventually a total of

Vickers Wellesley Vickers Wellesleys from 14 Squadron fly over the Pyramids. This two-seater bomber was in action well into 1942.

ten squadrons were to fly Wellesleys; while in January 1938 the RAF's Long-Range Development Unit (LRDU) was formed with Wellesleys at Upper Heyford especially to investigate the associated problems of ultra-long range flying. Here the design's overload Service range (normal) of well over 2000 miles was to be surpassed when two of an original flight of three LRDU Wellesleys left Ismailia, Egypt on 5 November 1938 and arrived non-stop at Darwin, Australia in the early hours of November 7 – a total of 7158 miles, and a new world distance record set to last seven years.

The outbreak of World War Two saw all Wellesleys in Bomber Command already re-placed by newer aircraft types, but three units already based in the Middle East, Nos 14, 47 and 223 Squadrons, flew their Wellesleys on highly active operations throughout the East African campaign and the opening rounds of the desert war in north Africa. By mid-1941 the monoplane's worthy frontline roles were over, but the design remains as one of the best interim aircraft flown by the RAF during its change-over from 'cloth' biplanes to metal monoplanes. Its undisputed 'proving' of the superiority of geodetic construction over more conventional structuring was to bear even more fruitful results with its stablemate, the classic Vickers Wellington bomber of revered memory.

Fairey Battle

The Battle was unfortunate in many ways. A clean, aesthetically-appealing monoplane bomber which, at the time of its conception, out-performed most of its rivals in most departments, the Battle was nevertheless under-powered and under-armed defensively for the daylight bombing role thrust upon its gallant crews in the first year of World War Two. The inevitable result was an appalling casualty rate – and, therefrom, a partly undeserved evil reputation fostered by many latter-day historians. Stemming from a 1932 specification, Battles first equipped 63 Squadron in early 1937 and were then over-produced – mainly for quasi-political reasons – with the result that by September 1939 Battles were being flown by no less than 15 squadrons of Bomber Command's total of 53 squadrons. Ten of those units comprised the whole equipment of No. 1 Group and all 160 Battles of this Group were despatched

to France on 2 September 1939. From the first clashes with the Luftwaffe it was clear to all but the obtuse that the design was totally inadequate for modern warfare, while the German *blitzkrieg* of May-June 1940 saw the Battle crews being massacred daily as they valiantly tried unescorted daylight bombing sorties against vastly superior opposition. Indeed, the first two airmen awarded Victoria Crosses in 1939-45 belonged to 12 (Battle) Squadron—both were posthumous awards. After withdrawal to England in mid-June 1940, the exhausted survivors were dispersed and the Battle faded rapidly from the operational scene.

Many hundreds of Battles were sold overseas, going to Australia, Belgium, Turkey, Greece

Fairey Battle A flight of Fairey Battles of 218 Squadron on patrol over the snow-covered French countryside in January 1940. This plane lacked the performance and fire-power necessary to combat the German fighters and was quickly withdrawn from service.

and South Africa, but the largest quantity—almost half of all Battles built—were sent to Canada to implement the Commonwealth Air Training Plan. H A Taylor, a wartime ATA pilot, making his first flight in a Battle, recorded 'The Battle was a strange but comfortingly English device. Little in the cockpit seemed to be logically arranged, but the various knobs and levers were all the more easily found and remembered for that reason . . . first of my memories is of the blast of hot air and dust from the heating system as the throttle was moved through the gate for take-off power and speed. The second memory is of the enormous drop in engine revolutions as the two-pitch propeller was moved to "fine" after the initial climb. The silence was almost complete as the engine speed dropped and the rpm needle swung back from 2900 to 1500 or so. Finally, there is the memory of the undercarriage, flap and bomb-door controls which sprouted out of the floor.'

Squadron Leader D H Clarke DFC, AFC is outspoken in his dislike of the plane:

It was born too late; it died early—but not early enough! Before it died it killed far too many damn good, fully-trained aircrew. After it died nobody regretted, nobody wept—nobody even noticed. Only those who flew it on ops—and survived—heaved a sigh of relief, but they were flying bigger and better bombers by then and couldn't care less.

And, let's face it—almost any bomber was better than the hideously ugly Fairey Battle which was neither nice to fly nor nice for ops. It lumbered and wallowed behind its spinnerless v.p. airscrew, incapable of reaching its designed top speed—in fact doubt was often expressed as to whether the darned thing had been designed, or whether the pre-war Hitler panics had caused the Air Ministry to rush into an order for one. I can only describe this ill-named aircraft thus: it was no fairy, and it just couldn't battle—except hopelessly.

Oh, it was built all right; certainly it was hulking-strong: the wing section near the roots was thick enough to conceal a 1,000 lb bomb. But the only thing in the wing which was offensive was one .303-inch machine gun—one! Plus another one for the poor devil of a rear gunner. And these were our front line bombers in France.

The pilot's cockpit was comfortable enough I suppose: it was roomy and had quite good forward visibility for an in-line engine; rear vision was poor. The rear gunner wasn't much better off: he had a tilting hood which screened his back from the slipstream, but because the backdraft curled in and slapped him full in the face, this was a useless gadget! The single rear gun had a poor arc of fire and the mighty rudder and tailplane effectively blocked most of it.

What is left? Well, the bomb aiming position was good fun—for a pilot who wanted to have a close-up view of what an undercart looked like when an aircraft landed. I used to enjoy doing this. As you lay face down looking through the oil-stained perspex panel and bomb-aiming gap, you had the short oleos and large wheels in full view. As the runway, or grass, came closer, and the surface blurred to streaky grey or green, you could swear that the bloke flying the kite was going to boob. Then, with no sense of stall, the wheels would meet the ground, smoke (on tarmac) would erupt briefly and the oleos would contract smoothly as they took the weight of the monster from its supporting cushion of air. That was always a fascinating performance. But I should have hated to have aimed bombs from that hole: the hot, oily stench from the engine made any stay in the prone position a sheer impossibility.

Hawker Hurricane I

No list of the world's greatest fighter aircraft could fail to include the ubiquitous Hurricane. The world's first eight-gun operational fighter, and the RAF's first squadron aeroplane able to exceed 300 mph with full warload; the Hurricane bore the brunt of the first nine months of the war in France where it gave the much-vaunted Luftwaffe its first taste of RAF opposition. In the Battle of Britain a total of 1715 Hurricanes were flown in combat at some period, more than the total of *all* other aircraft employed, and Hurricane pilots claimed almost 80% of all claimed victories by the RAF. In the following years 1941-45 Hurricanes gave splendid service on operations throughout the world, and in virtually every role possible for a single-engined fighter. Its battle honours included every theatre of war and facet of operations.

Hawker Hurricane I The Hawker Hurricane Is of 85 Squadron 'scramble' from an airfield at Merville in May 1940 at the height of the war in France.

One of the men who faced the numerically superior Luftwaffe from a Hurricane's cockpit throughout 1939-40 was Wing Commander Roland Beamont, CBE, OBE, DSO, who served with 87 Squadron in France. His view of the Hurricane came from hard experience:

In the spring and summer of 1940, although without the elegance and high altitude performance of the Spitfire, the Hurricane was a machine of its time, and many of us would not have changed it for any other mount. We knew it as a rugged, stable, forgiving aeroplane which was tolerant of our clumsiness and the worst that the weather could do. It absorbed legendary amounts of enemy fire and kept flying. We could hit the target well with its eight guns and when in trouble we felt able to outfly the enemy's best. The Hurricane and the Spitfire made a great team, but I never regretted my posting to a Hurricane squadron in that fateful time.

The Hurricane I with constant speed airscrew was a magnificent fighting machine, with excellent qualities of gun-platform stability, manoeuvrability up to 20,000 feet, ruggedness and ease of control on take-off and landing. In climb and level speed it was slightly slower than the Bf 109, but no more than 20-30 mph, which meant it was not always easy to

get away from a 109 – but that was not the object of the exercise. Once in combat the Hurricane could easily out-manoeuvre the 109. Above 20,000 feet the 109 was better; but when correctly employed against the bomber formations and close escorts

Bristol Blenheim I A Bristol Blenheim I from 211 Squadron attacks Italian troops at Klisura, Albania during the Greek campaign of late 1940.

below 20,000 feet the Hurricane was magnificent for the task. When in September 1940 there was talk in my squadron (87) of replacement by Spitfires there was nearly a riot—if our Hurricanes were 'inferior', no one had told us about it! This tremendous spirit and confidence in their aircraft was typical of Hurricane squadrons at that time. In direct comparison I found that the Hurricane could out-turn the Spitfires I and II at low and medium altitude, and could very easily do this to the Bf 109.

Bristol Blenheim I

A military variant of the Bristol Type 142 *Britain First* presented to the nation by Lord Rothermere, the Blenheim I medium bomber first equipped 114 Squadron at Wyton in early 1937. Its immediate ability to outpace any contemporary fighter established the 'short-nose' Blenheim as the RAF's fastest bomber of the pre-war years. Though soon to be replaced in UK-based squadrons by its development, the Mk IV 'long-nose' version, the Mk I Blenheim continued its operational service in the Middle East and India for several years; while converted Mk Is with four-gun packs added under the belly were flown operationally as night fighters during 1938-41. This latter variant helped to pioneer airborne radar and achieved a modicum of success against German night raiders during 1940-41. During the early stages of the Middle East campaigns, particularly in the Greek debacle, Blenheim I bomber crews played a significant part in the Allies' desperate defences against greatly superior odds and in relatively primitive maintenance and operating circumstances. Overall, no less than 54 RAF squadrons operated Blenheim Is at some period, apart from its operational use

Lockheed Hudson A Hudson from 206 Squadron on patrol over the beaches at Dunkirk during the evacuation of the Allied Expeditionary Force in May 1940. Although primarily a long-range reconnaissance aircraft in Coastal Command, the Hudson performed many other duties.

by several other foreign countries.

An ex-Blenheim I pilot summed his feelings about operating the type as a bomber, 'On the surface it was pleasant to fly, was certainly very manoeuvrable, and had few technical vices. Initial reaction – coming from Hind biplane bomber cockpits – was a feeling akin to a cramped goldfish, with all those window-frames surrounding one up front, but the pilot's view forwards, sideways and down was excellent in relation to take-offs or landings. One-engine landings could be dicey, but provided one remembered to maintain or increase critical speed limits a simple, steady circuit with the good engine on the inside of the turn usually produced a safe landing. The Blenheim's most evil characteristic – and it appeared to apply to all marks – was the minimal chances for pilot survival should he need to take to his brolly (*parachute*). I personally knew of three men who were forced to bale out, and each one was chopped up by the propellers.'

Lockheed Hudson

With the distinct possibility of war with Germany looming large in 1938, and mindful of the RAF's genuine need for advanced designs of aircraft in real quantities; Britain turned to the USA for possible sources of production aircraft. An original British Purchasing Commission (later retitled Mission) went to America in April 1938, and one of its purchases was a block order for 200 militarised variants of the Lockheed civil Model 14-F62 (to be named Hudson I for the RAF) as navigational trainers and eventual replacements for Avro Ansons. The first Hudsons for RAF operational use equipped 224 Squadron in mid-1939 initially, and a total of 27 squadrons plus numerous other units ultimately. Their prime role was with Coastal Command during the opening war years, in which they excelled relative to other twin-engined designs with similar duties. In later years Hudsons became festooned with radar antennae, rockets and other fitments as such items came into general use.

To RAF-trained pilots the American cockpit instrumentation appeared highly complicated with numerous knobs, levers and hand-operated devices scattered around the 'front office'.

This produced near-mesmerisation as was possibly summarised by H A Taylor, describing his first Hudson landing on a ferry trip:

While my right hand fluttered over the various levers on the throttle pedestal (a baker's dozen of them, in fact, not counting those for the undercarriage and flaps) I tried to remember all that I'd been told, rightly or wrongly, about this formidable aeroplane. Never use full flap . . . never trim it right back on the approach . . . motor it in to a wheeler . . . don't try to three-point it. These and other things (which escaped my memory) they had said. As the grass came up, instinct forced me to haul back on the control column in a valiant effort to make a 'proper' landing. The main wheels touched rather heavily . . . I pushed the control column hard towards the dashboard and waited. After an agonising second or two the wheels touched again, and then again – and stayed on the ground. Not my idea of a landing, but it seemed that the Hudson had, in its own way, duly arrived.

Ex-Aircraftman Fred Adkin recalls the Hudson:

The Hudson was a distinctive aircraft, having a large girth, twin fins and rudders, and a two-gun turret mounted very close to the tail unit. In accordance with my usual practice I took the opportunity to have a flip in one. The visibility was amazing from the turret, where it seemed as though one was perched high on top of the fuselage. The aeroplane was quite good to service, displaying the typical American flair for tidy and compact lay-out of services, compared with the British method of putting items as afterthoughts in any odd space available.

These aircraft were prone to an irritating and dangerous snag, that of excessive tailwheel shimmy, which sometimes caused them to swing off during

Supermarine Spitfire I

The Spitfire is now an international legend. Created by Reginald Mitchell and his Supermarine design team in the 1930s, it was the only Allied fighter to remain in full production from pre-1939 until after 1945. During those years more than 40 major versions and a host of minor variants came into being; an indication of the superb development potential of Mitchell's original brainchild. The prototype first flew in March 1936, and 19 Squadron became the RAF's first Spitfire unit at Duxford in August 1938. The change from obsolete biplanes to this sleek metal monoplane was summed by Adolph 'Sailor' Malan, DSO, DFC, who was with 74 Squadron then, 'It was like changing over from Noah's Ark to the *Queen Mary*. The Spitfire had style and was obviously a killer. Moreover, she was a perfect lady. She had no vices. She was beautifully positive. You could dive till your eyes were popping out of your head, but the wings would still be there – till your inside melted, and she would still answer to a touch.'

Malan was referring to the Mark I Spitfire, and it was this version which equipped Fighter Command throughout the Battle of Britain of 1940. Here its superior rate of climb and higher altitude performance made it an ideal partner to the more rugged Hurricane when tackling the armadas of Luftwaffe bombers and fighters attacking Britain. The confidence felt in their aircraft by all Spitfire pilots of 1940 was

encapsulated in the words of the late D M Crook, DFC, who flew the 'Spit' in the 1940 battles, 'Practically everybody who has flown a Spitfire thinks it is the most marvellous aircraft ever built, and I am no exception to the general rule. I grew to like it more than any other machine I have flown. It is so small and compact and neat, yet it possesses devastating fire power, and it is still probably the best, fastest fighter in the world.'

Group Captain J H Hill commanded a fighter squadron at the height of the Battle of Britain:
By mid-1940 I had spent several months in France as an Air Controller before being seconded to a Hurricane squadron to command it. I had only

Supermarine Spitfire I The Spitfires of 64 Squadron return to their burning airfield at at Kenley to refuel and re-arm at the height of the Battle of Britain. It was equipped with one Rolls-Royce Merlin III engine and had an armament of eight 0.303 Browning machine-guns.

about five hours flying time on Hurricanes, and unfortunately was shot down very early on, but managed to bale out and after returning via Dunkirk and a period in hospital, I had a quick refresher course on Spitfires and was sent to command 222 Squadron, then equipped with the Spitfire Mark I. Although I had hardly seen a Spitfire before, in a fortnight we were in Hornchurch in the thick of the battle, but by that time I had flown about fifteen hours and was quite happy as the Spitfire was a beautiful aeroplane to convert on to.

One of the most extraordinary features of the Mark I was the undercarriage lever on the right-hand side of the cockpit. It was a large piece of equipment resembling iron piping; when the aircraft took off the pilot selected 'undercarriage up' and had to pump this piece of ironmongery with the right hand. However, the Spitfire had extremely sensitive elevators. Consequently, when we took off in squadron formation, as we normally did, the planes would be seen to be 'porpoising' up and down – an effect of pulling and pushing the lever with the right hand while trying to keep the aeroplane steady with the left hand which normally controlled the throttle making quite an amusing sight. But the sensitivity of the elevators and the ailerons made it a beautiful aeroplane to fly.

Having flown both the Hurricane and the Spitfire, I feel it is true to say that one could not have had two better aeroplanes for their respective roles. The Hurricane was a slightly sturdier aeroplane and a more stable gun-platform whose role was to attack the bombers; the Spitfire was a dog-fighter that would get as high as possible as quickly as possible to keep the German fighters from attacking the Hurricanes lower down.

The Me109 was slightly faster than the Spitfire, especially in a dive. To counterbalance this, the Spitfire had the better turning circle and once in a dogfight, the Spitfire could get 'inside' the Me 109. In fact, the first Me 109 I shot down was when we were both upside down over St Paul's Cathedral. In that situation I discovered that I had much more control than the man ahead of me, and I'm fully certain he went down as a 'flamer'.

Gloster Gladiator

The Gladiator was the last biplane fighter to be used by the RAF's operational units, and though regarded by many as a 'peacetime' aircraft in fact Gladiators saw highly active service, first as fighters and later in 'backwater' roles throughout World War Two. Their true fighting heyday was from 1939 to 1941, during which period Gladiator pilots claimed at least 250 combat victories over such diversified war zones as France, Norway, East Africa, Egypt, Libya, Greece, Crete and Malta. Indeed, the highest-scoring Allied fighter pilot of the war, M St J Pattle, DFC, gained almost half of his 40-plus victories from a Gladiator cockpit. Entering service with 72 Squadron in early 1937, Gladiators formed the equipment of more than 30 squadrons or other front-line units, both at home and, particularly, overseas.

To one pilot who had spent several years flying open-cockpit fighters the Gladiator made a great impression, 'The claustrophobic feeling of being surrounded by a greenhouse canopy took some time to disperse. With the lid shut one felt like a goldfish. In flight the Gladiator was astonishingly easy to fly; very manoeuvrable and tight on the controls, with instant positive response. Admittedly, I had a good rigger to look after my kite, but I think most Gladiator pilots would probably say the same. The knowledge of having four instead of two machine guns was oddly comforting when we first took on the Luftwaffe, but despite the type's good speed and aerobatic qualities, we knew we were well outclassed by most opponents. As one officer put it, we were fighting World War Two with World War One equipment.'

Armstrong Whitworth Whitley

Unspectacular in design, performance and operations, the Whitley was a particularly rugged packhorse for the RAF from its introduction in 1937 until 1945. Despite its ungainly appearance – and due to the angle of its huge, thick wings, the Whitley always seemed to be flying with its nose well down – it shared with the Wellington and Hampden in spearheading

Gloster Gladiator One of Malta's famous Gladiators, which formed the nucleus of 261 Squadron's 18-day air-defence of the island. This was the last British biplane fighter and had many of the features that were to become commonplace, such as an enclosed cockpit, flaps and a simpler undercarriage.

Bomber Command's night offensive over Germany during the first three years of World War Two. Thereafter it served in many roles; coastal reconnaissance, glider-tug, paratroop carrier and trainer. Individual OTU Whitleys were still flying occasional bombing sorties over France as late as 1944. Many outstanding bomber captains in the latter years of the war cut their teeth on Whitleys, and the aeroplane

Armstrong Whitworth Whitley Whitley Vs
of 51 Squadron drop propaganda leaflets over
Germany in 1940. This five-seater heavy
bomber had a maximum bomb load of
7000 lb, and was one of the mainstays of
Bomber Command at the outbreak of war. It
was phased out as a bomber from 1942 to
become a glider-tug.

established many firsts in Bomber Command
annals during 1939-41. Its hefty construction
absorbed astonishing damage on occasion, yet
Whitleys suffered the least casualty rate among
their contemporaries on operations.

From a pilot's viewpoint the Whitley was, as
one put it, 'A strange device for the uninitiated.'
Requiring very firm handling generally, it was
nevertheless very stable. On take-off or landing

it had a tendency to 'float' for lengthy periods, a trait which – combined with the unusual wing angle in relation to the fuselage – gave many inexperienced pilots some unnerving moments during first flights. Once its idiosyncrasies were understood, the Whitley offered dependable, patient qualities well appreciated by most of its early bomber crews.

Vickers Wellington

The 'Wimpy' – its universal nickname which derived from a pre-1939 newspaper Popeye strip cartoon featuring a chubby, hamburg-eating trencherman named J Wellington Wimpy – was the real mainstay of Bomber Command during 1939-42, and remained on active operations throughout the war. As with its predecessor, the Wellesley, the Wellington framework was of lattice-work geodetic construction, fabric-covered, and this offered surprising strength. It also permitted somewhat alarming flexing of both wing and fuselage to pilots fresh to the design. Having accumulated a prodigious record as a bomber by 1942, the Wimpy was then to give great service with Coastal Command in the unceasing war against German U-boats, and by 1945 maritime

Wellington crews had sunk or at least seriously damaged a total of 51 enemy submarines. Outside the European war zones, other Wellingtons gave trojan service in the Middle and Far East theatres.

In flight a Wellington was never exactly placid; wings and tails seemed to have a strong desire to flap, controls tended to wander of their own accord in the cockpit, and wing fabric ballooned alarmingly with decreasing air pressure at altitude. Nevertheless, on becoming accustomed to a Wimpy's inherent quirks, pilots found them pleasant, forgiving machines to fly, with relatively good powers of manoeuvrability if made to undertake mild aerobatics. Extensive development was attempted with the Wellington, including a drastically revised Mark VI version which had a pressurised cabin for the pilot and a separate pressurised cocoon for the tail gunner. From it was also developed the Warwick; a 'stretched' Wimpy eventually adapted mainly for air-sea rescue duties.

The following are extracts of correspondence we have had with Group Captain W S O Randle, Keeper of the Battle of Britain Museum:

No-one can question that the Wellington ranks amongst the great aircraft of all time. For my part, I was one of the fortunate many who can look back with affection on the Wimpy, as most of us called her, which occupied the first seven years of my flying career. It was also my good fortune to see at close quarters the first Wellington, the B9/32 prototype, K4049, rightly regarded as the most advanced design of its day, in the New Types Park at the Hendon Air Display in 1936. Now, working at the Royal Air Force Museum, I can daily visit

MF628, the sole survivor of the thousands of Wellingtons which served the Royal Air Forces.

After training, my crew and I joined 150 Squadron at Snaith, which was equipped with the new Mark III, with its more powerful Hercules engine and wooden fully-feathering propellors. We arrived there on 8 July 1942 and on 23 July in X 3313 my crew and I went on our first trip, to Duisburg. Most of our flying was at night and a considerable proportion of it in cloud; I found the Wellington relatively easy to fly accurately on instruments and by no means tiring. She was also manoeuvrable for a bomber and could corkscrew under certain circumstances well within the turning circle of an approaching fighter. Her durability was renowned and 150 Squadron had its full share of

Vickers Wellington Ground crews from 99 Squadron, then based at Waterbeach, Cambridgeshire, prepare Wellington Mark IC bombers for a night operation in the winter of 1940. This Mark had a range of 2200 miles, a ceiling of 22,000 feet, a bomb-load of 1500 lb, and a maximum speed of 235 mph.

aircraft returning with damage which in another type would probably have meant loss or destruction.

We flew X 3313 fairly regularly, until I was given BJ 877 to fly. This aircraft, lettered Z-Zebra, was the only one on the squadron modified to carry the 4000 lb blockbuster. The standard bomb-beams and doors had been removed and the large bomb was held by a single shackle with about one quarter of this dustbin-shaped weapon hanging *clear of the aircraft. The flying characteristics of the modified aircraft were noticeably different. With a much heavier load held around the centre of gravity, she was less stable, and because of the drag of the exposed part of the bomb, a little slower. There was no need to confirm 'Bomb gone' as, upon release, the aircraft seemed to bound upwards and then, much lighter, she became more manoeuvrable and, if anything, faster. It was in this aircraft that I stumbled upon cruise climbing and thereafter held her in a trimmed climb right to the target area. It was not unusual to be at 20,000 feet crossing the Dutch coast and as high as 23,000 feet over the Ruhr.*

The overriding concern for all at Snaith was for Z-Zebra and its crew to get off the ground safely with its odd load. We were always the last aircraft to take off for fear that a disaster on the runway could put the Station out of action before the squadron was airborne.

In the early hours of September 16 we went mine-laying off Wangerooge at the mouth of the Elbe and that evening returned to Germany en route to Essen. Over Zwolle on the Dutch coast, at 21,000 feet with a strong following wind of more than 100 knots, we were hit with a solitary anti-aircraft shell. About fifteen minutes later, the port engine failed and we feathered it. We were then descending into the Ruhr barrage and at about 16,000 feet Z-Zebra was hit by flak a second time. With full opposite rudder and the wheel hard over to keep the wing up, she could only manage to fly in a large erratic circle, being blown by the strong tail wind further and further into Germany. We baled out and the only unusual happening was the start of what must have been a barrel roll by the Wellington as I let go of the controls.

The normal number of crew in a Wellington was five, but on this occasion we had a passenger. Our Wireless Operator was captured and spent the next three years in a Prisoner of War Camp, but the rest of us returned to England over a period of about six months, and I believe that this was the first almost complete crew to return home. My evasion and that of the rear gunner and of the passenger was due to the excellent services provided by a Belgian Escape Route.

I last flew a Wellington in August 1948, and the aircraft disappeared from service soon after. MF628, at Hendon, is the sole survivor of the 11,461 built.

North American Harvard

From 1938 to 1955 the noisy Harvard was a standard instructional vehicle for the RAF, and was responsible for conveying the art of 'real' flying to numberless thousands of embryo air crews. Usually nicknamed the 'Yellow Peril'–a reference to its normally all-yellow training livery–the Harvard was always immediately recognisable in the air by its harsh, rasping tone akin to dry linoleum being torn hastily. Though not unstable, the Harvard needed constant flying from take-off to landing; a valuable asset in that it ensured total concentration by student pilots while airborne. The layout of the controls was distinctly American, with a daunting array of instrumentation facing the new 'driver' on his first Harvard solo. Its long 'glasshouse' perspex canopy offered excellent vision fields, while its manoeuvrability permitted instruction in aerobatics to a high degree; a necessary adjunct to any advanced trainer.

As H A Taylor said, 'Things had to be done properly and in the right order. A "drill" was required and its routine flying and handling had necessarily to be left largely to pre-trained reflex action. It was for the Harvard that we were taught one of the school's most valuable little tricks–a kind of mnemonic for the cockpit drill. Throughout six years of war, while flying maybe 50 or so different aircraft types, this mnemonic worked. With a few modifications and additions it could be used successfully even for monsters like the B-24 Liberator bomber.'

Squadron Leader Clarke was familiar with the Harvard during the last years of the war:

The comfortable front cockpit, not too roomy, not too small, with sufficient knobs, instruments and gadgets to make you feel that you were pretty clued up knowing what they all did. The rear, instructor's, cockpit was perhaps more stark and the visibility not nearly so good, but you soon got used to splay-eyed hold-offs instead of the old fashioned hang-your-head-over-the-port-side method of landing. The instructor was comfortable enough in the back, but the real enjoyment came when he was solo—in the front.

The formidable and characteristic external blare of the Pratt and Whitney Wasp was a muted sewing machine to the pilot's ears, yet it gave a reasonable punch in the back for take-off and had enough reserve to make continuous aerobatics

North American Harvard A pupil pilot under instruction brings a Harvard in to land after a training flight. As for all instructional aircraft, the Harvard was painted bright yellow to ensure maximum visibility.

possible without losing height. Ailerons, rudder or elevators; stalling, high-speed stalling or spinning; flaps, undercart or pitch—whatever you used or did, in or with the Harvard it was positive, easy and emphatically safe. Apart from the steerable tail-wheel which pupils sometimes, somehow, managed to unlock by ruddering over forty-five degrees whilst landing (which inevitably resulted in a ground loop, but with no more damage than a dented wing tip), the Harvard was more snag-free than any

other kite of equivalent or better performance – and
a good deal better than the majority of slower
aircraft!

So . . . I practised for hours to take the Harvard
to the limits of its wide safety margins – partly
because I enjoyed practising, partly because I had
to do some special work, partly because I rather
fancied myself as an aerobatic pilot in 1945.

The special work was using a Harvard virtually
as a helicopter. As CI of the OTU at Fayid I
took it upon myself to be responsible for rescuing any
'red-on-black', 'forget-to-switch-over-tanks' or
'started-pinpointing-when-the-ETA-was-up'
pupils. There were plenty of 'em – quite apart from
the more excusable, but just as frequent reason
when our war- and OTU-weary Spits and Kittys
gave up the ghost on the Course triangular across
country or at any other time – generally the most
inconvenient. Then, everybody (and by that I mean
Instructors, not – Allah preserve us! – pupils) got
airborne and square searched the vastness of sand
until the unfortunate pranger was located.

Desert landings on soft sand, hard sand, rock,
small plateaux or wriggling wadis taught me that a
Harvard, if pressed, could take off in fifty yards and
land in fifty feet – that is, with an average windspeed
of ten mph. Undoubtedly this sounds like a line, but
I expect that there are still a few bods who will
remember the occasions when I used to land on the
compass base at Fayid, touching down and stopping
inside the marked circle of cardinal points. The
whole secret was to descend near-vertically with the
stick back, stalled (fifty-five on the clock); then,
undershooting and just before touching down,
slamming the throttle wide open for a couple of
seconds to check the fall. The result was spectacular,
dangerous for one's rank in the event of the engine
missing even for a second (the undercart would have
gone straight up through the wings, and my
superiors through their respective ceilings), but
very necessary to pick up those pupils who might
otherwise have had to wait sometimes for days before
being rescued.

Bristol Blenheim IV A Blenheim IV of 114
Squadron on a low-level bombing run over
the power station at Knapsack, Cologne in
1941.

Bristol Blenheim IV

The first RAF aircraft to penetrate German skies in World War Two was a Blenheim IV (N6215) of 139 Squadron, on a reconnaissance sortie from Wyton on 3 September 1939; the next day Blenheim IVs of 107 and 110 Squadrons carried out the RAF's first bombing sortie by attacking German ships in the Schillig Roads. In effect a 'stretched' Blenheim I, having extended nose accommodation for the observer/navigator/bomb aimer, the Blenheim IV saw a high degree of operational use during the years 1939-42 in most theatres of war. Usually operating by day, the Blenheim IV crews of No. 2 Group, Bomber Command are particularly remembered for their dauntless courage in returning to the fray almost daily during 1941-42, despite appalling casualties. More than 60 RAF squadrons flew the type at some period until being superseded by more modern designs.

The many hydraulic and other engine controls in a Blenheim—mostly esoterically designed and located by its makers including their own design of the mid-upper power-operated turret—could be frustrating to a fresh pilot; particularly the many similar-looking plungers and handles, and the two-pitch propeller controls which were placed *behind* the pilot's seat location. Once airborne, however,

the aircraft was easy to operate, with few real vices. Surprisingly compact for a bomber, the Blenheim IV could lift a bomb load of some 1300 lb over a range of 1300 to 1400 miles. Defensive armament—as with so many other pre-1939 designs—was inadequate for daylight operations; comprising merely two guns in the dorsal turret and, inexplicably, a single fixed forward gun for the pilot.

Handley Page Hampden

Six years old in concept, and incapable of significant development, the Hampden stood worthily alongside the Whitley and Wellington as the spine of Bomber Command at the outbreak of war in 1939. And until the advent of bigger, four-engined bombers in 1941-42, the Hampden soldiered on valiantly, maintaining the RAF's main offensive capability against Germany despite its patent obsolescence and totally inadequate defensive armament. Even then, after being replaced in the bomber role,

Hampdens continued operations with Coastal Command as torpedo bombers until late 1943. Cramped crew accommodation—the internal fuselage width was a mere three feet—increased crew fatigue over any extended sortie; yet the 'Flying Suitcase' was ever popular. To an astonishing speed range from 73 mph landing to 260 mph maximum, was added extreme ease in handling and fluid manoeuvrability. Sitting high, with an unmatched field of vision, a Hampden pilot could handle his bomber almost

like a fighter. As one pilot expressed his own experience, 'It was a delightful aeroplane to fly. The aileron control was brisk and tight turns were a special pleasure . . . and if you were prepared to take a little trouble with the business of landing, it offered the kind of landing that made one's day.'

The 'wring-out' capability of a Hampden is perhaps exemplified by the occasion when the late Grahame Ross, DFC, at Aston Down OTU in 1940, engaged two Spitfires in a friendly dogfight with surprising results for them, 'Both Spit pilots were amazed at my Hampden's aerobatics and had to pull out all the stops, and even then had great difficulty in getting even a passing sightline on me.'

Handley Page Hampden The Handley Page Hampdens of 408 'Goose' Squadron of the Royal Canadian Air Force are prepared for a night-time mine-laying mission. The 'Flying Suitcase' was fast and manoeuvrable, but had inadequate armament and was underpowered, with only two engines.

Boulton Paul Defiant

The ill-starred Defiant was unique on its introduction to the RAF as being the Service's first fighter fitted with a power-operated gun turret as its sole armament. Its design conception envisaged its use for attacking enemy bomber formations from the beam, but in early 1940 when Defiants first flew into combat, it was used as a normal fighter – with disastrous results. Despite early optimistic claims of combat successes, the Defiant crews soon suffered devastating casualties, and by August 1940 the type was relegated to night-fighting duties.

Fitted with early Airborne Interception (AI) radar, the night Defiants proved relatively successful during the German night blitz of 1940-41, but were superseded in the role by

Boulton Paul Defiant A Boulton Paul Defiant night-fighter from 255 Squadron, based at Kirton-in-Lindsey, searches the moonlit sky. The Defiant was outclassed as a daytime fighter but was a capable night-fighter; the observer in his power-operated turret could constantly scan the upper sky and shoot down bombers from below or beam-on.

Beaufighters thereafter. For the rest of the war Defiants served as training target-tugs, while a number gave valuable service with the newly-created Air-Sea Rescue organisation.

Pilots generally liked the Defiant from a pure flying viewpoint. The front cockpit was relatively roomy, and visibility forward better than in most in-line engined aircraft of the time. In the air it tended towards heaviness on the controls. As one pilot explained, 'She was as solid as a rock in a dive, built up a lot of reserve speed through her weight, and was nice near the ground. If anything it handled rather more like a bomber than a fighter.' Another ex-Defiant crew member has recorded, 'The Defiant was well liked for its reliability, good handling qualities, lack of vices and simplicity for flying and landing at night.'

Squadron Leader Clarke expressed the general combination of satisfaction and frustration that pilots felt about the Defiant:

There were two rear-gun fighters in World War 2: the Blackburn Roc and the Boulton Paul Defiant. They were both armed with the same Boulton Paul turret which fired four .303 Brownings, which rotates through 360 degrees (they automatically cut out in the appropriate places so that the gunner could not shoot off the prop, tail or rudder!), and which was so accurate that the maker's expert could insert a pencil in one of the muzzles and sign on a piece of board held in front of the guns.

There was only one snag. Whoever invented the rear-gun fighter completely forgot to invent how it could attack anything! You just couldn't attack unless you ran away – and if you ran away how could you possibly call the thing a fighter?

From the pilot's point of view the Defiant was a reasonable enough aircraft. Heavy perhaps, with a very definite relationship towards the Hawker Hurricane – so much so that the one outstanding victory achieved by Defiants was when a gaggle of 109's jumped twelve of them from out of the sun and ran into the concentrated fire of forty-eight .303's – but without inheriting the rather poor top speed of that over-praised fighter and most certainly without approaching its manoeuvrability. The

Defiant handled more like a bomber than a fighter.

The cockpit was roomy enough and as well equipped as most British wartime fighters; in other words the pilot soon realised that 'things had been added', and nine times out of ten they had been put in the worst possible place. Still, the visibility forward was better than average for an in-line engine, and it was obvious that the rear gunner could warn the pilot about the E/A coming up astern.

The rear gunner was really the most important person on board, and if the Defiant had made the grade there is no doubt that PBO's would have re-created the importance they justly earned in World War I. But apart from that one glorious massacre they did not have a chance, and the Defiant became a jack-of-all-trades.

It was a great shame that the Defiant had been cursed with a rear-gun turret from birth! If only she had been fitted with 40 mm cannons firing forward – and she was big enough and seemingly strong enough to take them – and with a couple of 250 lb armour-piercing bombs, I think she would have achieved a lot of success as a ground attack aircraft. She was as solid as a rock in a dive – a wonderful front gun platform; she built up plenty of reserve speed; she was nice near the ground.

Supermarine Walrus

A 'Shagbat' is, according to Service legend, an ancient Egyptian bird able to fly in ever-decreasing circles – with a logical conclusion to its flightpath. It was also the nickname for the Walrus amphibian. Originally a private venture design by the 'father' of the immortal Spitfire, R J Mitchell, the Seagull V – its original title – was adopted as the Walrus from 1935 by the Fleet Air Arm as a spotter-reconnaissance aircraft able to operate from land, aircraft carriers or, via a catapult, from individual ships of the Fleet. For the next ten years the Shagbat served its masters faithfully, accepting a myriad of unlikely tasks in a bewildering variety of circumstances and climates around the globe – and never failing to uphold its ubiquitious roles as a naval jack-of-all-trades. By 1945 its

Supermarine Walrus A Supermarine Walrus Air-Sea Rescue amphibian picks up a crashed pilot from the English Channel in 1941. This was a development of the Supermarine Seagull and was a very angular single-engined biplane. The slab-sided fuselage hull was made from sheet aluminium alloy.

prodigious Service record had earned it the unofficial Service motto: 'Where there's a war, there's a Walrus'. Apart from its outstanding maritime honours, the Walrus became from 1941 an increasingly welcome sight to many hundreds of RAF and USAF crews forced to ditch in the sea. Its use for air-sea rescue duties gave birth to many mini-epics of cool courage by Shagbat crews as they alighted in mine-infested enemy waters to retrieve Allied airmen.

A noisy, underpowered anachronism on the aerial scene of 1939-45, nevertheless the Walrus was always regarded by those who flew in it with high affection. Indeed one FAA pilot, B J Hurren declared, 'Excepting possibly the Swordfish, one may doubt whether any aeroplane in any Service in the world has a record in war which can match the old Shagbat.'

Short Sunderland

The last, and unquestionably the queen of all flying boats to be used in RAF squadron service, the Sunderland was much more than merely a good aeroplane to its crews; it was a war chariot, home and bed and board for countless air crews who preferred to live aboard their aircraft between sorties rather than revert to the more normal Service domesticity of Mess and bunk ashore. Its RAF life began in May 1938 and it was not until May 1959 that the ultimate Sunderland in RAF livery flew the type's final sortie. Between those dates Sunderlands ac-counted for some 60 U-boats sunk or damaged in World War Two, flew as mercy angels evacuating hard-pressed Allied troops from hazardous situations, airlifted vital supplies into Berlin during the late 1940s, operated over the Malayan jungles and seas during *Operation Firedog* in the 1950s, and participated in the Korean war.

Vic Hodgkinson, DFC, who flew Sunderlands during and after the war described the Sunderland as:

Short Sunderland A Short Sunderland I of 210 Squadron undergoes engine maintenance while at its moorings. This was arguably the best flying boat of World War Two – its monoplane configuration and aerodynamically cleaner fuselage were clear improvements on predecessors such as the Walrus.

. . . a dream to fly – very stable (probably due to the high wing) and the deep hull giving no pendulum effect. Ailerons and elevators were light finger-tip control, and the rudder a little heavier; though as with most heavy aircraft in the air this latter was not used much. We normally cruised at about 120 knots and around the 4000 feet mark. Synchronising engines was done by setting up the two inners by ear – then looking along the props and adjusting the outers until the 'shadows' stopped. The Aldis Lamp was sometimes used for this purpose by night. I flew Marks I, II and III Sunderlands and there was no difference between any of them from the flying point of view. If you can call it a difference then engine handling was the one.

Supermarine Spitfire V

The Mark V versions of the Spitfire not only predominated in Fighter Command's squadrons' equipment in 1941, but were built in greater quantity – a total of 6479, or almost 30% of all Spitfires ever constructed – than any other Spitfire variant. The Mark V offered three main forms of armament. The Va carried eight .303 Browning machine guns; the Vb a mixture of two 20 mm Hispano cannons and four .303 Brownings; while the Vc could be fitted with either of these 'batteries' or alternatively be fitted with four 20 mm cannons plus carriage of a 500 lb bomb under the fuselage. All Mark V versions had a more powerful engine than their Mark II predecessors, and were able to engage the newly-introduced Messerschmitt Bf 109F of 1941 on roughly equal standing. Many though by no means all Mark V Spitfires were instantly recognisable by having 'clipped' wing-

tips; though later variants also employed this particular modification for low altitude roles.

The introduction by the Luftwaffe of their Focke-Wulf Fw 190 fighter by mid-1941 came as a shock to Allied air authorities, and the new German fighter quickly proved itself well superior in most facets of combat performance to the Spitfire V. The result was the introduction of the Spitfire Mark IX, built in quantities only second to the Mark V in the Spitfire story. The Mark V was also the first Spitfire type to be tropicalised, and served in the North African campaign and other Mediterranean zones of operations. It remained in production for some two years supplying several hundreds of examples to the Royal Navy and to Australia.

Supermarine Spitfire V Spitfire Vb's of 303 (Polish) Squadron take off from Northolt to make a sweep across the Channel in 1942.

Flying Officer M Ferić was one of the Polish pilots of 303 Squadron based at Northolt. This is an account of one of his first dogfights in a Spitfire:

Kellett's flight split up and each of them selected one Me 109. What about us? We did not have to wait long for a job. Another flight of three Me 109s, flying much higher than the first, came to the rescue of their comrades. They dived down and were passing in front of us, as we were some 300 yards behind our first flight. That was lucky, especially as one of the Huns was already firing at

Sergeant Karubin, who was busy with the Me 109 ahead of him. Wunsche took him on. I went after the other, putting on full throttle. I caught up with him easily, he grew in my sights until his fuselage occupied the whole luminous circle. It was certainly *time for firing. I did it quite calmly and I was not even excited, rather puzzled and surprised to see that it was so easy, quite different from Poland when you had to scrape and try until you were in a sweat, and then instead of getting him, he got you.*

Hawker Hurricane II

While the Hurricane I bore the lion's share of the RAF's fighter campaigns from 1939-41, the quest for heavier armament and, if possible, better performance for the design commenced in late 1938. First thoughts included the installation of 12 Browning machine guns in the wings, up-rated Merlin engines, and fitments externally for extra fuel tankage to increase fighting range. This version, the Mark IIb, began to reach RAF squadrons in mid-1941; but a much more lethal armament of four 20 mm cannons followed in the Mark IIc. This was in turn followed by the IId, armed with twin 40 mm anti-tank guns under the wings; while other Mark IIs were introduced with under-wing rails for three-inch rocket projectiles and/or carrier-borne bombs. All such variants had entered squadron service by the close of 1942, and many were destined to continue on operations until the end of the war serving in every war theatre in Europe, the Middle East and the Far East. Hurricane IIs were also given to Russia—nearly 3000 in all—

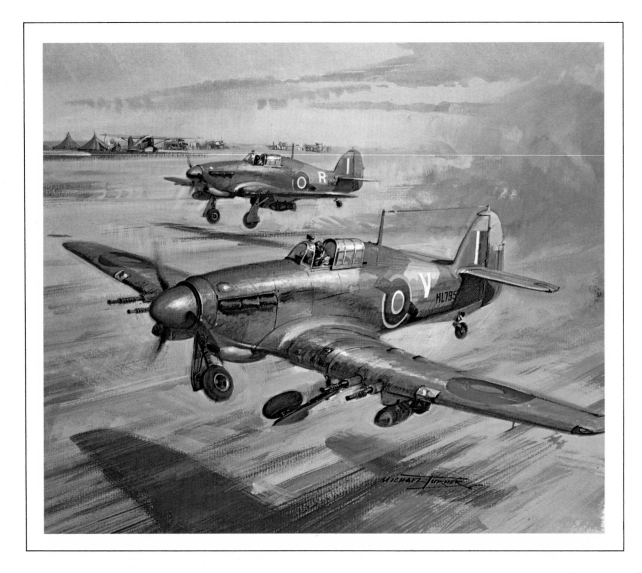

representing slightly more than a fifth of all Hurricanes ever built.

Fred Etchells, who flew Hurricanes for more than four years from Britain and in various Middle East campaigns, has summed up his own feelings:

Although superbly manoeuvrable despite slightly heavy controls, we had to admit reluctantly that the Hurricane did lack speed, but I don't think I ever heard a word spoken against the aircraft. Somehow one loved the Hurricane without either realising or expressing it, and it was only after flying Spitfires with controls light enough for a five-year old to handle that one came to realise the strength required to throw a Hurricane about the sky.

Hawker Hurricane II Hawker Hurricane IIc fighter-bombers from 274 Squadron take off from a desert airstrip in North Africa in 1942. In comparison to the Mark I (see pages 69-72) it had a more powerful engine (the 1280-hp Merlin XX), a two-stage supercharger and heavier armament.

Westland Whirlwind Fighter

The Westland Whirlwind was designed to perform the two duties of long-range escort and night fighter. It possessed an extremely heavy offensive capability with four cannon mounted in the nose, and entered service in June 1940. However, the aircraft suffered from serious defects. The Whirlwind's two Rolls-Royce Peregrine engines were both unreliable and low-powered, and in addition the aircraft had a very high landing speed of 80 mph that made it impossible to use on grass airfields. Eventually a mere 112 Whirlwinds were built and were used only in 137 and 263 Squadrons.

What little success this aircraft had was as a fighter-bomber on cross-Channel bombing and strafing sorties. Its range was 800 miles; its maximum speed was 360 mph (without bombs).

Westland Whirlwind Fighter Westland Whirlwinds of 263 Squadron, operating from Filton, on patrol near Bristol early in 1941. This single-seater fighter or fighter-bomber was designed as a twin-engined high-performance aircraft, but arrived in service too late to be effective and was swiftly phased out.

Bristol Beaufort

Pilots' reactions to the ungainly Beaufort torpedo bomber varied. Peter Geldart, undergoing a conversion course to Beaufighters, had no great opinion of the type, 'The Beaufort I with two 1010 hp Taurus engines was a hopelessly underpowered aeroplane, incapable of maintaining a straight and level flight on one engine. However, how they flew these machines on operations with an 18-inch torpedo slung underneath her I shall never know – I only know I'm pleased I was not asked to do it.' Pat Gibbs, DSO, DFC, possibly the leading torpedo specialist of the RAF then, was less scathing but no less respectful of the Beaufort's characteristics, 'The Beaufort, although completely without vices, was something of a handful and demanded respect . . . it was not

Bristol Beaufort The Bristol Beauforts of 42 Squadron, Coastal Command, launch a torpedo attack on an enemy convoy in 1941. The Beaufort was a four-seater torpedo bomber that was derived from the Blenheim (page 72) and in turn gave rise to the Beaufighter (page 105).

docile and demanded constant and vigilant supervision. This first impression that a Beaufort required always to be consciously flown and never left to its own devices, particularly near the ground, is one which I have never since found reason to modify. The aircraft had to be flown right from the start of the take-off until it had actually stopped running at the end of the landing run. To enter a shallow dive was to see the needle of the airspeed indicator rapidly cover the 200-knot scale, pass the 300 mark, and still continue upwards.'

First entering service with 22 Squadron in late 1939, the Beaufort became the RAF's standard torpedo bomber until 1943, albeit being used more as a day bomber. Ten squadrons were eventually equipped with the type, operating mainly in European or Mediterranean waters; but some 700 machines were built in Australia and operated over the Pacific with RAAF units.

Roy C Nesbitt flew Bristol Beauforts in 217 Squadron, Coastal Command from January 1941 to March 1942:

I joined the RAFVR in September 1939 and trained as an air navigator, being commissioned when aged 19 in January 1941 when I joined 217 Squadron and began flying on Bristol Beauforts. There were only three Beaufort Squadrons at that time: 22, 42 and 217. I completed 49 operational flights, 217 Squadron being based successively at St Eval in Cornwall, Thorney Island in Hampshire and Wick in Caithness. During my operational service, the squadron lost 24 Beauforts, the normal operational strength being no more than 10. I left the RAF as a First Lieutenant in 1946.

Originally designed as a torpedo bomber for Coastal Command, the Bristol Beaufort also fulfilled a variety of other roles, such as dive bombing warships and merchantmen, low level attacks on ports, mine-laying and anti-submarine and other patrols. These sorties could vary from fairly safe to suicidally dangerous.

The Beaufort was an immensely strong aircraft, but it was heavy and difficult to fly and there were many accidents on training and operational work. Even after modification of the early Taurus engine,

only a very skilful pilot could maintain height on one engine. Later, the Wasp engine proved far more reliable, for if one engine was hit during an attack the pilot could feather the propellor and reduce the risk of fire, whilst there was a good chance of getting home on the remaining engine.

A crew of four manned the Beaufort. The pilot sat on his parachute in a bucket seat on the left-hand side. Beside him was a co-pilot's seat where the observer sat on take-off or landing. For the remainder of the flight, the observer sat by a chart table in the perspex nose, which was also equipped with a bomb sight. Behind the pilot was an armoured bulwark and then the wireless operator with his large Marconi transmitter/receiver and direction finding equipment. The gunner sat in a mid-upper or dorsal turret, which could traverse sideways and aft, but not forwards.

The Beaufort carried 2000 lb of bombs, consisting of two 500 lb enclosed in the bomb bay and four 250 lb suspended from wing racks. Alternatively, it carried a torpedo, land mine or sea mine of about 1750 lb protruding from the bomb bay. The pilot operated a single forward-firing Browning .303 in the wing, later increased to two. The turret was at first equipped with a single drum-fed Vickers K303, later increased to two, and later still to two Browning .303s. The wireless operator often carried two Vickers Ks, which he could mount in the port and starboard waist hatches.

Although the Beaufort achieved some success as a torpedo and dive bomber, losses could be extremely heavy when flying at low level in the face of

intense flak, and Beaufort crews were often considered to have the highest mortality rate in the R.A.F.

De Havilland Tiger Moth

From 1932 until 1947 the 'Tiger' was primarily responsible for elementary flying instruction of virtually all RAF air crews, and was also the last biplane *ab initio* trainer used by the RAF. It was a cold, draughty machine in which to fly; it had no brakes but an efficient, forgiving undercarriage which saved countless would-be pilots' pride and was surprisingly tough in view of the rough handling meted out to it by ham-

fisted student 'drivers'. In the air the Tiger was fully aerobatic and could be 'wrung out' with complete confidence in its inherent strength of

De Havilland Tiger Moth A de Havilland Tiger Moth ready to start-up at an Elementary Flying Training School in the summer of 1942. This was the last biplane trainer to be used by the RAF. Over 8800 Tiger Moths were built and many can still be seen flying today.

construction; though for reasons still not fully explainable, slow rolls were always difficult to achieve neatly. Indeed it was said, 'If you can roll a Tiger, you can roll anything'.

The basic design remained virtually un-altered throughout its long, patient service, though many Tigers flown in Canada were provided with an enclosed canopy for their open cockpits to combat the icy temperatures of the Canadian winters. Slightly more than 8800 Tigers were eventually built, and many privately-owned examples are still in evidence today—living tributes to a fine aircraft and to the affection in which the type is still held by those who prefer 'real' flying.

De Havilland Mosquito

With the golden advantage of hindsight, it could be said that the superb Mosquito—always 'Mozzie' to its crews—came into being *despite* the Air Ministry. Conceived in 1938 as a private venture, its all-wood construction and lack of defensive armament—the latter in deference to the design's high speed for evading attack—was officially considered too unorthodox for Service use. Delays in official sponsorship meant that the first prototype did not fly until November 1940, but by mid-1941 the aircraft's superlative performance earned it full-scale production orders. Considering that one of the earliest Mosquito bombers, with full load, outpaced a Spitfire V which was using emergency boost, it is worthy of speculation as to what effect on the overall bomber offensive of 1941-45 might have been created had the Mosquito been accepted for full bomber production from its inception in 1938. Postwar statistics indicate that Mosquito crews flew roughly four times the number of sorties per aircraft loss than the equivalent ratio in Lancasters.

Few RAF aircraft have escaped condemnation from some quarter on their introduction—but the Mosquito was certainly one. From 1941 to 1945 Mozzies undertook many roles: recon-naissance, bomber, fighter, anti-shipping scourge and submarine hunter and destroyer. All were facets of the Mosquito's versatility. Whatever its role it retained a fighter-like performance, an aerobat's fluid agility, and a ruggedness which absorbed terrifying damage, yet still delivered live crews from the wreckage. Syd Clayton, DSO, DFC, DFM, who flew 145 sorties as both navigator and then pilot, said of the 'Wooden Wonder', 'I'm obviously biased regarding the Mossie but as a pilot I found her a wonderful aircraft which would take a severe hammering and still fly on one engine.' Frank Ruskell, DFC, a navigator, summed up his feelings, 'The Mosquito was a good-looking aeroplane of high performance. It seldom let you down . . . you could not help loving it and went to war in it with every confidence.'

As Wing Commander Anderson OBE, DFC, AFC said in his book *Pathfinders*, whereas *a Lancaster taking off gives the impression of tremendous power hauling a ponderous weight triumphantly into the air, a Mosquito taking off rather suggests a bundle of ferocious energy that the pilot has to fight to keep down on to the runway. The place to watch is from the end just where the Mozzie gets airborne. You see her starting towards you along the flarepath, just a red and green*

De Havilland Mosquito The Mosquitoes of 105 Squadron carry out a low-level raid on the marshalling yards at Ehrang on 1 April 1943. The aircraft's cruising speed was 325 mph at 13,000 feet, its ceiling was 33,000 feet. The Mosquito was originally a two-seater fighter-bomber but was used in a number of other roles of which the most important was photographic-reconnaissance. 7781 Mosquitoes were made before production ended in November 1950.

wingtip light. Soon you can distinguish her shape, slim and somehow evil, and suddenly she is screaming towards you just like a gigantic cat. A moment later she is past and thirty feet up in the air.

Avro Lancaster

This was, indisputably, the finest night bomber of World War Two–some would even argue it was *the* best bomber of those years. Originally projected in 1939 as the Avro Manchester III, the Lancaster began arriving in Bomber Command in late 1941, and from 1943 was the RAF's principal heavy bomber. More than 7000 were built, and some 70 squadrons flew the type at some period. With rare exception all men who flew in Lancasters praised the aircraft, while its increasing adaptability for heavier and more complex warloads as the war progressed became a byword. By 1945 specially modified Lancasters were capable of lifting 12,000 lb and 22,000 lb bombs–something never accomplished by other RAF bombers. Excluding No. 100 Group, Bomber Command's strength in April 1945 showed approximately 67% were Lancaster-equipped units.

Jack Currie, who flew Lancasters on operations with 12 Squadron, said of the aircraft, 'The Lancaster looked good because everything was well-shaped and in proportion and she had a good flying attitude . . . in between take-off and landing the Lanc flew herself. She was a dream aeroplane.' Another veteran bomber pilot who completed two tours of operations recalls, 'My first tour of ops was on Hampdens and how I survived unscathed I'll never know.

Avro Lancaster Lancaster Path Finders have dropped their colour-coded markers (green in this case) to pinpoint the target, and the Lancs of 57 Squadron follow them in to release their bomb-loads. The golden trails are fire from automatic weapons, but these rarely reached as high as the Lancasters.

Yet when I was next posted to a Lancaster squadron for my second bite of the cherry, I felt no apprehension. The Lanc's reputation was already spreading round the air crews, and after my first test flight in her I *knew* I'd survive – such was the confidence this beautiful bomber inspired. Throughout 30 sorties she never once failed me – despite several distinctly hairy trips when flak and Jerry fighters punctured her liberally—and her Merlin engines always functioned perfectly. If one can love a hunk of metal, I certainly loved the Lancaster.'

Leading Aircraftman Cliff Allen was one of the many ground crew without whom it would have been impossible to keep the aircraft flying. Here he discusses servicing the Lancaster:

Those who have never climbed up the wheel of a Lanc to reach the engine priming positions have missed out on life! Port and starboard-inner engines each had their own priming station, while also on the same panel was the connection for the plug to the trolley ace. It required some agility to swing up the wheel and get both feet on the footrests situated halfway up the oleo legs. Many were the antics performed in the pitch black of night, sometimes during atrocious weather conditions: to get positioned for start-up, rubber boots slipping on greasy untreaded tyres, produced lots of foul language. The ideal situation at start-up was for one man to perch behind each primer, with another seated on the trolley ace. The latter job was usually carried out by our rigger whilst a bod for signalling to the pilot may have been the NCO if available; many would be the occasion when only two men filled this duty.

Bristol Beaufighter

They called it 'Whispering Death' in Burma, while in Britain and the Mediterranean theatres the Beaufighter was renowned for its brute-like strength and ultra-lethal punch of four 20 mm cannons and six Browning machine guns—the heaviest armament battery fitted to any RAF fighter of World War Two. A brilliant adaption of its stablemate the Beaufort, the first Beaufighters were issued to the RAF's nightfighter units in 1940 and 1941, but in time the aircraft came to be used in many other roles. In the Middle East its low-level performance as a ground-strafer was put to good effect, and in Coastal Command Beaus formed the original strike squadrons for the vital anti-shipping offensive role. In the latter task the Beau was soon adapted to carry torpedoes, rocket projectiles and/or bombs in addition to cannon or gun armament. From October 1942 Beaufighters began to arrive in the Far East and remained on operations there until several years after the war.

George McLannahan flew Beaufighters and said of them:

I found the Mark I a strong and powerful machine but very tiring to fly on patrol at night, or on instruments, as it was completely unstable fore and aft. This was virtually cured on the Mark VI.

I came onto the mark VI after flying Mosquitos and it was like handling a battleship after being used to a destroyer. On this aspect an American in 153 Squadron who had joined the RCAF (Royal Canadian Air Force) early on to get into the war commented that he felt completely at home in a Beau as he'd previously been a truck driver! Rather unfair on the Beau as it was a very fine, solid aircraft. For just one example, landing it in a cross-wind was never a problem; once placed properly on the ground it sat there and defied any deviations.

One of the most effective roles of the Bristol Beaufighter during World War II was against enemy shipping. Group Captain R E Burns,

CBE, DFC and bar, commanded 254 Squadron and earlier in the war the Aircraft Torpedo Development Unit. He was extensively involved in these operations and in the technical advances in the aircraft torpedo with which the anti-shipping variant of the Beaufighter – known as the Torbeau – was equipped:

The first entry of the Beaufighter into Coastal Command was to counter the German long-range aircraft which were attacking our convoys in the North Atlantic. Focke-Wulf 200 Condors were four-engined aircraft that both attacked our merchant shipping and provided reconnaissance for the positioning of German U-boats. The Beaufighter had long range and endurance and

Bristol Beaufighter Bristol Beaufighters of 254 Squadron, Coastal Command, attack enemy flak ships with cannon and torpedoes. The aeroplane shown is a 'Torbeau' that has dropped its torpedo and has continued over the enemy ship. The forward pair of shackles that carry the torpedo can be seen underneath the pilot's cockpit.

terrific fire power and could knock these rather slow aeroplanes out of the sky, but it clearly had potential for other roles within the Command.

The appearance of a very much improved aircraft torpedo equipped with a gyroscopically controlled tail – the MAT Mark IV – that controlled the flight of the torpedo in pitch and roll after release, offered a useful weapon which was fully commensurate with the speed, performance and flexibility of the Beaufighter enabling these characteristics to be fully exploited in the anti-shipping role. This combination of aircraft and weapon produced the Torbeau.

The idea of the specialised Anti-Shipping Strike Wings had evolved earlier as a means of countering the German Navy, but implementation had been delayed because of conflicting demands overseas for the types of aircraft, trained crews personnel and equipment such Wings would require. In the event the Beaufighter Strike Wings entered the field too late to have any marked impact upon the activities of the German Fleet which had by then been effectively neutralised. They were however employed with great success against enemy merchant shipping, denying to the Germans the free movement of men, material and equipment crucial to the war effort.

The German war industry was vitally dependent upon high-grade iron ore. This was mined in Northern Sweden, transported by rail to Narvik and then shipped down the Norwegian, German and Dutch coasts on its way to the Ruhr. The Swedes, on their part, were desperately short of coal and a reciprocal trade in iron ore, coal and coke—essential to both countries—considerably increased the flow and importance of shipping between Norway and the ports that supplied the Ruhr. Additionally the Germans had a large garrison in Norway which had to be supplied and maintained by sea.

To meet this situation Coastal Command had by late 1943 deployed three Beaufighter Wings: two in Scotland and one south of the Humber at North Coates in Lincolnshire. Nominally the Scottish-based Wings operated off the Norwegian coast while the North Coates Wing took care of enemy convoys sailing west of the Elbe. In practice rigid lines of demarcation were not drawn and one Wing might be called upon to carry out strikes in another's area. Sometimes two or all three Wings would join forces to act in concert against an exceptionally large convoy.

In response to air attack in general the Germans had operated their shipping in convoy and later provided them with anti-aircraft escort vessels or 'flakships'. The ratio of flakships to merchantmen steadily increased as our attacks became more and more successful and by early 1943 was about 3 : 1

and still increasing. A flak escort ship of the trawler type might mount six to eight guns, at least one being an 88 mm and the rest 37 mm and 20 mm guns using some form of course and speed sight while the 'M' class minesweepers which came to be employed in increasing numbers in support of convoys were even more formidably armed.

A typical German/Dutch coast convoy consisting of, say, four merchant ships would probably have at least twelve escorts. The merchantmen would be found sailing in line ahead with the escorts deployed about 1000 yards on either beam. Preceding the convoy would be the minesweepers.

Our primary target was the merchant ships and our objective would be to get three or four torpedo-carrying aircraft to within the 1000 yards dropping zone of each of these. A force of torpedo aircraft acting on its own against such a strongly defended target could not hope to be successful let alone survive. It was necessary therefore to suppress the flak during the crucial period while the Torbeaus were getting into range and carrying out the aiming run to release their torpedoes.

After experimenting with various tactics for suppressing the flak the essential close synchronisation was achieved quite simply by flying a combined force of anti-flak and torpedo-carrying Beaufighters into the attack as a single formation, maintaining a set height and distance between the two elements during the final approach to the target.

The Wing Leader—generally someone who had served an apprenticeship as a torpedo pilot—would endeavour to position the whole formation so as to get the Torbeaus into the optimum situation for their torpedo run on to the merchantmen. On the order to attack—given over the R/T—individual Beaufighters of the anti-flak sections would dive down from their approach height of about 3000 feet on to their preselected targets among the flakships. Below at 250–300 feet above sea level and about 1000 yards behind, the Torbeaus would manoeuvre in their tactical sub-units to develop their torpedo run on to the merchant ships.

The torpedo-carrying Beaufighter and the 'flak-buster' were identical aircraft to the Torbeau specification. In the torpedo role an 18 inch torpedo with a 550 lb Torpex warhead was carried. Instead of the torpedo the 'flak-buster' was equipped *with a battery of rocket projectiles under each wing and relied on these and the four forward-firing 20 mm cannons to discourage the enemy gunners.*

It was seldom worthwhile for the torpedo pilots to fire their guns during the attack or possible to do this effectively since the torpedo run, in spite of the less taxing conditions permitted by the improved torpedo with the MAT Mark IV tail, nevertheless demanded more or less straight and level flying at 250-300 feet. The extent to which losses were sustained during this period depended on how well the 'flak-busters' were doing their job.

Firing the cannons in a Beaufighter upset the residual magnetism in the aircraft and the compasses went awry. In order to rectify this situation – if only partially – you had to get onto a northerly heading as soon as possible after leaving the target area and fire a burst. Alternatively you could follow someone home who had not fired his guns – a torpedo pilot for instance.

The German convoys were generally fairly easy to find since they followed their coast line, only venturing as far out to sea as was necessary to get the required depth of water under their bottoms. This was normally the 6-8 fathom line on the charts. Off the German and Dutch coasts, where enemy fighter opposition might be fiercest, this fact put the convoys 10-15 miles out to sea. This was an advantage to us since it reduced the early warning time available to the enemy. Also we invariably flew in very low to keep below the radar horizon and thus maintained the element of surprise for as long as possible.

Incidentally the Torbeau was equipped with a dihedral tailplane which considerably improved longitudinal stability for torpedo work and long flights at very low altitude over the sea. As we seldom operated above 500-1000 feet except when developing an attack or in the circuit oxygen equipment was never used and was eventually removed to reduce weight. The two Hercules engines were rated for optimum performance at low altitude.

With determination a Torbeau could be wound up to produce a sea level speed in excess of 300 knots after an attack and this often made it difficult for the Messerschmitt 109s. The Focke-Wulf 190s were more worrying since they had the performance to stay with you and make repeated attacks.

We did have a rear gun in the Beaufighter but this was more of a 'scare' gun than an effective weapon. It had a very narrow arc of fire on each side of the tail fin but strangely enough it did seem to deter the German fighters who were reluctant to come in from dead astern and preferred the beam attack which was less accurate.

The anti-shipping Beaufighter had a two-man crew and the rear gun was operated by the navigator who already had a lot to do since he also operated the W/T and of course did the navigation. Additionally, when under an attack from a fighter the navigator would provide a continuous commentary for his pilot on the fighter's position and estimated range. When he thought the fighter was about to open fire he would warn his pilot who would initiate a violent corkscrew turn into the direction of the attack. This was often very effective. A coolheaded navigator was worth his weight in gold.

Supermarine Spitfire IX

The debut of the Luftwaffe's Focke-Wulf Fw 190 in mid-1941 and its patent superiority over the Spitfire V led to a hasty remedy by the RAF. The Spitfire VIII – a Mark VII with Merlin 61 engine – was already planned, but Fighter Command requested an interim variant which could be brought into service more quickly as an answer to the Fw 190. The resulting Mark IX was basically a Mark Vc, with a Merlin 61 engine, identifiable by its twin radiators and four-bladed propeller. The Mark IX first entered service in July 1942 with 64 Squadron based at Hornchurch, and was in combat before that month was out. It introduced a new combination of armament, having two 20 mm cannons and two 0.50-inch machine guns, plus the capacity for carriage of up to 1000 lb of bombs. The Merlin 61 of 1660 hp had a two-speed supercharger and raised the Mark IX's top speed to slightly more than 400 mph. In the

Supermarine Spitfire IX The Spitfires of 127 Wing led by Wing Commander Johnnie Johnson strafe an enemy airfield during a sweep over Northern France in 1943. This was in essence a Mark Vc with a more powerful engine.

event the success of this supposedly interim variant led to its production in greater quantity (5665 aircraft) than any other form of Spitfire except the Mark V, and the Mark IX remained in operational squadrons until 1945. More than 100 squadrons flew Spitfire IXs at some stage.

Hawker Hurricane IIc (Far East)

By 1942 the Hurricane was patently outmoded for fighter operations in Europe, but its operational life was by no means ended. Many were despatched to the North African campaign and for the defence of besieged Malta, where they added considerable laurels to an already proud battle record. In the Far East Hurricanes were destined to figure largely in the early disastrous months of the Japanese onslaught in Malaya and Burma, but were then to provide a rock

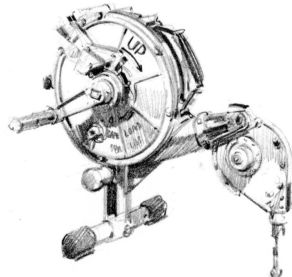

Hawker Hurricane IIc (Far East) The Hurricanes of 60 Squadron acting in support of the 11th East African Division bomb and strafe Japanese troops retreating along the Tamu Road in Burma.

foundation for the long struggle which culminated in ultimate defeat of Japan in 1945. By June 1943 a total of 23 squadrons in India and Burma were equipped with Hurricanes, almost exclusively Mark IIs plus a few Mark IVs. Bearing clutches of bombs, rockets and cannons, Hurricanes proved to be deadly effective in their main role of close support over the battle areas for the jungle-bound infantry. By late 1944 most Hurricanes in Burma had been replaced by the seven-ton Thunderbolt for tactical back-up to the army, but on VJ-Day (15 August 1945) at least eleven squadrons, including the Indian Air Force, were still operating Hurricanes.

Appreciation of the Hurricanes' prodigious efforts are the words of a contemporary report, 'The army displayed an enthusiasm for the Hurri-bombers as of no other combat aircraft in the India-Burma theatre. From the despatches of commanding generals to the private mail of the men fighting in the jungle, have come messages of praise for Hurri-bomber attacks pressed home at the appropriate moment. It is the proud boast of the pilots that they never failed to give prompt aid when called upon by their comrades fighting on the ground.'

Westland Lysander

Conceived in World War One, the role of army co-operation was considered essential enough to justify a series of aeroplanes specifically designed for this task in the following two decades, and for the RAF to designate complete squadrons to such duties. Westland's high-wing Lysander–or 'Lizzie' as it was commonly called–was the first monoplane in RAF service to undertake the role, and in the event the last to be designed solely for such a purpose. First issued to 16 Squadron in June 1938, Lizzies eventually equipped more than 30 squadrons and other special units. Seeing brief but gallant action in France and the North African campaigns of 1940-41, the Lysander was then relegated to more mundane but no less vital roles such as target-tugs, air-sea rescue, and general communications liaison. Specially adapted versions, however, played a secret 'cloak and dagger' role from 1941 to 1944, transporting and retrieving Allied secret agents to and from Occupied Europe.

Bearing in mind its original design conception, the Lysander was admirably suited to its role. Pilots sat high with an excellent all-round downward field of vision, while the aircraft's slow speed characteristics offered landing runs said to be no longer than a cricket pitch. A heavy landing was occasionally known to shake loose the weighty Mercury engine from its holding bolts, but when treated with average respect a Lysander was considered a pleasant, restful machine to operate.

Group Captain Vaughan-Fowler flew the Lysander extensively:

My first introduction to the Lysander was in November, 1941 at RAF Old Sarum where the Army Co-Operation Operational Training Unit was based. Having finished my advanced training on Hurricanes I was not looking forward to regressing to some aircraft that looked as though the Science Museum was clearing out its old stock. How wrong my original thoughts were. Some three years and 800 hours later I had–hnd still have–a tremendous affection for an aircraft which had taken me and not a few passengers in and out of some fairly odd places.

One's first approach to the aircraft was slightly daunting. To get into it required two steps to reach the top of one of the wheels and then a rather complicated climb up the wing strut and into the cockpit which sat some ten feet above the ground. From this vantage point a very good downwards view was obtained. The main difference in the controls from other aircraft of the time was the elevator trimmer. This changed the angle of incidence of the tail plane and could be lethal if the aircraft was taken off with landing incidence still selected; this was achieved by winding a wheel on the left of the seat. Another similar wheel on the right of the seat raised and lowered the seat. This could also cause embarrassment at times; if dive bombing was being carried out and the seat was not in the fully up position you found yourself plummeting to the bottom of the cockpit when high G-forces were applied.

I was able to fly the Mark I, II, III and IIIA. They were all very similar except for the engines. The Mark I had the Bristol Mercy XV rated at

15,000 feet and with only a two speed propeller it had to be throttled back above 10,000 feet so as not to exceed engine speed limitations. The Mark II had the Bristol Perseus, a sleeve valved engine; not too successful and not many were built. The Mark III had the derated XX and XXX Bristol Mercurys and the aircraft used for special operations also had the Rotol variable pitch propeller allowing for more economical operation.

The other main difference from contemporary aircraft were the slats which stretched the full length of the wings. The outer slats came out as speed was progressively lowered below 85 mph. The inner slats started out at 65 mph. They were interconnected with the flaps and landing in very windy and gusty conditions could be rather an adventure with flaps coming up and down as the inner slats went in and out. The undercarriage was immensely strong and was made from a one piece N-shaped girder imported from Switzerland. In high wind conditions the slats would also let the aircraft descend in a fully stalled condition, apparently vertically – a slightly unnerving sight from the ground but a useful attribute when approaching a small field over high obstacles.

As a 'wartime wonder' Army Co-op trained pilot, I always admired those pilots who could produce a perfect 'vertical line overlap' set of photographs, direct a battery of artillery using a Morse Key and fly the aircraft without getting lost in the process. No onboard computer, data link and moving map display for them, only the original Mark I eyeball!

The fixed front guns, which were mounted one in each of the undercarriage spats, were temperamental. I don't believe anyone ever achieved a completely empty ammunition tray. These were in the fuselage immediately below the pilot and the ammunition was fed down the undercarriage struts to the guns. This always led to a jam after a few bursts. When the

Westland Lysander A Lysander prepares to take off from a field in Occupied France. The aircraft entered service as a two-seater army co-operation aeroplane, but during the war was given a multitude of tasks. Its most surprising achievement was as a fighter – the first Heinkel 111 to be shot down over BEF territory was downed by a Lysander in November 1939.

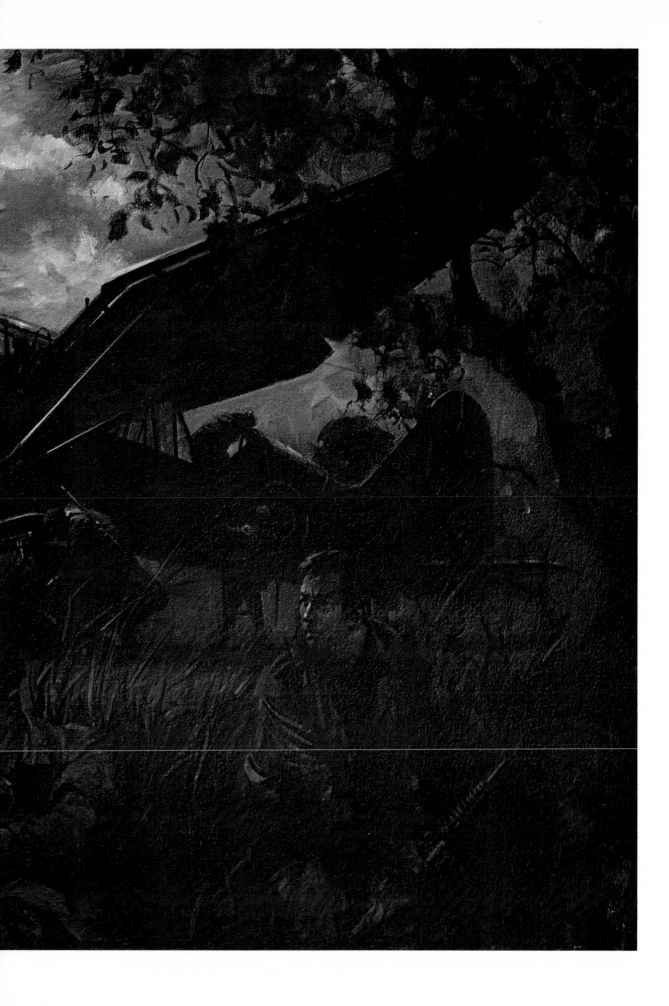

aircraft was used on special duty operations at night the whole armament system was removed to save weight.

The main modification to the special duty aircraft was an additional 150-gallon petrol tank slung under the fuselage. This tank had originally been designed as a fuselage tank from the Handley Page Harrow (page 62) and had nothing more than a self-sealing coating wrapped round it and a nose and tail cone fitted to give it some semblance of streamlining. This, together with the standard 98-gallon internal tank, gave the Lysander an endurance of 10 hours. Not to be recommended; as even after 7-8 hours one's back side became pretty numb from sitting on the standard single seat dinghy pack!

My main connection with the Lysander was over two years on special operations operating into France from the UK and into Greece, Yugoslavia and France from Italy and Corsica. If I describe one of the more difficult trips it will, perhaps, best underline the sterling qualities of the aircraft. Squadron Leader Hugh Verity (author of We Landed by Moonlight*) and I were detailed for an operation (code-named* Floride*) near Chateroux in the middle of France. Cloud base was 200 feet and raining when we left Tangmere on the night of 21/22 July, 1943 and remained thick and low for virtually the whole trip. By that time in our tour of operations we were fairly experienced and we*

had to fly on instruments most of the time breaking cloud just before coming to our major check points like the French coast, the River Loire and the target area where there were a number of easily recognised water land marks. The return was similar and about 6½ hours later we arrived back at Tangmere with seven passengers including a mother and her two children. I noted at the time that we were the only two aircraft to leave the UK on operations that night. It would have been impossible for any other aircraft to manoeuvre in such poor visibility and low cloud base let alone land in a 600-yard field. One of the more bizarre episodes of this period was a landing on a flare-path of three candles! The Gestapo had surprised the reception party the day before and they were unable to replace the torches that had been abandoned.

This has been a very limited account of one aspect of the Lysander's career. It remained on operations until the end of World War Two doing work which was not uppermost in the designer's mind back in 1934. It is a proud record for it carried close to one thousand very special passengers to and from operations in Europe and the Far East during the course of the war. With our pilots its reliability was legendary—never once did it let us down in Europe, but I must also stress that, in large measure, a good piece of equipment is only as reliable as those looking after it—the unsung ground crews.

North American Mitchell

Used in relatively small numbers by the RAF—only six squadrons within Bomber Command—the North American Mitchell was excellent for its purpose of day-bombing, which was its major role with No. 2 Group and later 2nd Tactical Air Force (TAF). Relatively fast, well armed defensively, and able to lift bomb loads between four and six thousands pounds, the Mitchell came into squadron service from September 1942 and was still operational at the close of the European war. In American use the B-25—its USAAF title—was built in greater numbers than any other twin-engined bomber, and its many variants gave sterling service in

many war zones, particularly in the Pacific. Few crews found serious cause for complaint in the Mitchell. Docile to handle with good control responses, highly manoeuvrable for its size—its wing span was almost 68 feet—and with a dependable tricycle undercarriage; the Mitchell was popular as a war vehicle.

One pilot who flew Mitchells with 98 Squadron RAF—the first RAF unit to receive the type—recalled, 'The Mitchell was my first three-wheeler and "converting" to this seemingly frightening American monster with its new-fangled (to me) undercarriage gave me tummy tremors initially. On my first taxying-

North American Mitchell North American Mitchell IIs from 180 Squadron on a daylight bombing mission over Northern France in 1943. Named after the American bombing pioneer Billy Mitchell, this light bomber was made in greater numbers than any other American twin-engined combat aircraft.

out to the runway, however, I was delighted with the tremendous amount of vision I was enjoying all round. Take-offs and landings soon proved uncomplicated, while in the air I quickly got used to the mass of instruments, levers, knobs and handles which (to me) seemed at first daunting. It was the first aircraft I had flown where I actually felt in real command of the aeroplane.'

Consolidated Catalina

Protection of Britain's vital mercantile supply lines – the 'Battle of the Atlantic' – was a prime responsibility for the Royal Navy and the RAF's Coastal Command *every* day and night of World War Two. The RAF's utter lack of truly long range aircraft in the opening phases of this maritime struggle meant seriously inadequate air deterrent cover for the merchant ship convoys, and this deficiency was hastily filled by various measures including the introduction of several American aircraft types. One of these was the Catalina, a pre-war US Navy design, which entered RAF squadron service in early 1941. The 'Cat's' 4000 miles' range offered a prospect of mid-Atlantic aerial cover for convoys, and it later formed the equipment of ten coastal squadrons based in the UK; a further 12 squadrons flew Catalinas in overseas commands, mainly around the Indian Ocean.

Consolidated Catalina A Consolidated Catalina of Coastal Command attacks a U-boat in the North Atlantic. It was armed with six 0.303 Vickers K (sometimes Browning) machine guns.

Vultee Vengeance

Looking, at first acquaintance, rather like an overgrown Harvard, the American-designed Vengeance spent a relatively long time in reaching operational service. Designed specifically as a tactical dive-bomber in 1940-41, initial production examples did not fly until mid-1942, and it was to be a further year before RAF Vengeance crews first flew to war in the type. Though conceived at a time when the dive-bomber was considered to be a vital key to success – a result of the Junkers Ju 87 *Stuka* myth – by 1943 it was recognised that such aircraft were vulnerable without local air superiority; hence the Vengeance's RAF use was restricted to the India/Burma theatre of operations, where it equipped four squadrons and commenced war sorties from mid-1943. In action the Vengeance proved highly effective in pin-point

Vultee Vengeance Vengeance dive-bombers from 45 Squadron, based in India, peel off to attack a target in Burma in late 1943. The Vengeance could be highly effective but, like all dive-bombers, needed a fighter escort.

dive-bombing attacks and low-level strafing sorties against the Japanese army and its jungle communications' systems; albeit still requiring a Hurricane or Spitfire top cover escort on most occasions. Apart from its operational use overseas, the Vengeance was mainly used in the RAF as a target-tug for aerial gunnery instruction.

Handley Page Halifax

As the RAF's second four-engined 'heavy' to become operational in World War Two–it followed the Stirling closely but preceded the Lancaster–the Halifax soon acquired an evil reputation among squadron crews which lingered long after any such stigmatism was justified. By 1945 the Halifax's war record was a proud saga, rivalling that of the Lancaster in many respects. Successively modified and improved in the light of experience, the 'Hally' paired with the much-publicised Lancaster as the RAF's two principal weapons in the night offensive against Germany from 1942 to 1945. Elsewhere the Halifax contributed significantly to Coastal Command's anti-submarine campaign, it fought in the North African struggle, acted as glider-tug for the airborne invasions of Europe, ferried supplies and secret agents into enemy-held territory, and undertook a dozen

other little-known yet vital roles. The early variants' chief defect was an inability to maintain a safe operating altitude on operations, but this was cured with the Mark III version with its Hercules radial engines.

Lettice Curtis, one of the many female pilots of the Air Transport Auxiliary (ATA) who ferried all types of aircraft to the squadrons, said of the Halifax, 'It was the heaviest of the three wartime four-engined bombers to handle –one could not afford to let it get out of trim– and application of aileron could call for a certain amount of brute force. RAF pilots who flew the Halifax were normally taught to make wheel landings, touching down on main wheels with tail wheel well off the ground. This reduced the chances of a heavy landing in difficult weather conditions, at night or when the aircraft was heavily loaded. ATA, however, were

trained to make three-point landings which, in a Halifax, called for accurate judgment, since the change of incidence between flying and ground attitude was considerable, and full power was unlikely to help if the final hold-off was too high.'

The ground crew were of course an essential part of the RAF team. Wing Commander William Anderson OBE, DFC, AFC paid this tribute to them in his book *Pathfinders*:

These RAF ground crew may not be very impressive to look at. They are dirty and unkempt, for aircraft are messy, oily things. Their pockets bulge with spare parts, and weird tools stick out of their uniforms in unexpected places. And their

Handley Page Halifax A Halifax B III of 425 'Alouette' Squadron, Royal Canadian Air Force, leaves its dispersal point at Tholthorpe for a night raid on Germany late in 1944. This Mark had a greater wing span than earlier versions (from 98 ft 10 in to 104 ft 2 in) and four more powerful engines.

language is a wonderful thing to listen to. Yet though they are not and in fact cannot be spit-and-polish men, yet, they represent one of the greatest miracles of the war-time RAF.

Only a few months ago all but one had been civilians who had never seen the inside of an aircraft. Yet here they were responsible for the day-to-day upkeep of an incredibly complicated modern bomber. And so good was their work that night after night the bomber would go out, and the question of breakdown, apart from the effects of flak or cannon or icing, just was not considered by those that flew. For example, a trip to Milan that involved lifting a staggering load of bombs over the Alps was always considered a 'gift', a 'piece of cake'. The danger from flak or fighters was negligible, and the danger of failing to return for mechanical reasons just never entered into the calculations. And that is a measure of the confidence that air crew placed in the faithful care of the ground crew.

One of the secrets of this success, though the dirty mechanics would look at you pretty blankly if you suggested it, was pride. The ground crews were proud of their job, proud of the fact that the machine they were looking after might be going to Berlin that night to help smash Hitler. So they treated their aircraft as if she were their own, and indeed, in their heart of hearts I think they believed that she was. At least, she was a concrete expression of their hatred of the Hun. So they tended her with loving care. They would patch the bullet holes with pride. They would paint up a bomb on the side of the fuselage to mark each operation. And they would watch anxiously how the crew to whom their aircraft was loaned for the night handled their child. And a heavy landing jarred them even more than the people inside, and their faces in dispersal were heavy with reproach. Sometimes their aircraft failed to return after an operation. They would be sorry about the crew but the crew were so alive when they saw them last that it seemed impossible for them to be dead. But they would feel badly the loss of their aircraft.

Consolidated Liberator

The B-24 Liberator is universally recognised for its huge contribution to the USAAF's daylight bombing assault on Germany during 1942-45. What is not usually realised is the additional

Consolidated Liberator Liberators of 356 Squadron head for their home base at Salbani, India after a bombing mission in Burma. The Liberator had a wing-span of 110 ft, a length of 67 ft 2 in and a height of 18 ft.

examples flew with Transport Command in the latter stages of the war.

Allied crews' reactions to the Liberator varied. One pilot, after his first flight in the type, called it '. . . a big, cumbersome gormless pig'. Nevertheless, with more experience he, like most pilots, came to regard the Liberator more kindly. Another pilot recorded, 'It was a great aircraft to fly and had almost no vices. Easy to handle and reliable. It was stable, had good range, a good turn of speed if required, excellent visibility for spotting submarines, and was an excellent instruments-flying aircraft.' A third called it, 'The most comfortable aircraft for the pilot I've ever flown. The console was beautifully laid out insofar as control access was concerned, and the seat wonderfully adaptable with about four different adjustments . . .' No one ever regarded the Liberator as a graceful aeroplane. One pilot described take-offs in it as '. . . a charge forward, flailing with all its might, and eventually getting airborne in sort of an overburdened way . . . and then became a flying brick that did everything in close to flying attitude, more or less.' Yet one pilot, whose experience ranged from Tiger Moths to postwar jet fighters, called the Liberator 'A gentleman's aircraft'.

war record of the type in RAF and other Allied air forces during the same period. Slightly more than 2000 Liberators saw service with the RAF alone, and many of these went to Coastal Command as VLR (Very Long Range) submarine-hunters over the Atlantic battle-area. Indeed, these maritime Liberators accounted for 100 U-boats sunk or seriously damaged – slightly less than a third of all U-boats accounted for by RAF aircraft. Other RAF 'Libs' saw plentiful action in the Middle East and over Burma and India, while some modified

Martin Baltimore

A direct development of the Martin Maryland, the Baltimore was produced specifically for the RAF, and first production examples began reaching Britain in October 1941. Their subsequent war service was confined to the Mediterranean area, where Baltimores entered operations with 55 and 223 Squadrons in early 1942. For the following three years Baltimores were prominent in every Allied campaign in the Middle East, and in addition to nine RAF units were flown by two Royal Australian Air Force (RAAF) and three South African Air Force (SAAF) squadrons. In all, some 1500 Baltimores were produced for the RAF.

Some of the earliest Wright-engined Baltimores issued to 60 Squadron SAAF for photo-

reconnaissance were ill-received. To quote one unit pilot, 'They were not a patch on the Marylands being heavy and clumsy, though more powerful. Their Wright engines gave much trouble and couldn't stand up to desert conditions like the Pratt & Whitneys of the Maryland.' Later marks, fitted with the much more reliable Pratt & Whitney powerplants, were popular with their bomber crews, however, despite the cramped accommodation in the deep, narrow fuselages. The sheer strength of construction in a Baltimore paid dividends, especially during the latter war years when daylight formations of 'Balts' ran gauntlets of fierce, accurate anti-aircraft fire in target areas. such as Northern Italy.

Martin Baltimore Baltimore IVs from 223 Squadron approach their target in Northern Italy in 1944. This aircraft was a development of the Martin Maryland and had been produced specifically for the RAF, reaching Britain in October 1941 and serving around the Mediterranean until the end of hostilities.

Republic Thunderbolt

The Republic P-47 Thunderbolt–more usually termed 'T-Bolt' or 'Jug' (after Juggernaut)–was built in greater quantity than any other American fighter of World War Two; was the heaviest single-engine fighter in general operational use–it weighed twice as much as a Spitfire; and achieved its greatest fame as a long-range bomber-escort and low-level ground-strafer with the USAAF in Europe from 1943 to 1945. A total of 830 Thunderbolts were ultimately transferred to the RAF, the first to reach squadron use being the initial examples received in May 1944 by 135 Squadron in India. Subsequently a total of 16 RAF squadrons flew the 'Jug'–all in the Far East between 1944 and 1946. The climatic conditions over the Burmese jungles tended to

Republic Thunderbolt A Thunderbolt II of 134 Squadron taxies out on to a flooded airstrip in Burma late in a 1945 monsoon. This was the heaviest single-engine fighter at that time; as can be seen, it needed a very deep fuselage to accommodate the supercharger and ducting.

exaggerate both the good and less favourable qualities of this ultra-heavyweight among fighters. On balance, however, the aircraft's poor rate of climb and turn over Burma were more than compensated for by its diving stability, high altitude manoeuvrability, and mainly trouble-free engine. A particular bonus was the design's ruggedness and sheer brute strength, which was blessed by every pilot who had to force-land or even crash-land.

The Thunderbolt's cockpit was ever a thing of wonder to British pilots more used to the tiny near-claustrophobic cabins of Spitfires and Hurricanes. As one RAF P-47 pilot quipped, 'In the Jug boredom on patrol was never a problem – one could always pass the time merely counting instruments and levers, or simply get out of the seat and have an invigorating run round the joystick . . . !'

Douglas Boston

Despite its outmoded defensive armament – the dorsal gunner had merely twin hand-operated machine guns – the Boston was in many other ways greatly superior to the Blenheim IV which it replaced in squadron service with No. 2 Group, commencing in the autumn of 1941. The Boston was also the RAF's first tricycle-undercarriage bomber to see general operational employment. Mike Henry, DFC, an air gunner, has recorded his first impressions of the Boston. 'What a magnificent aeroplane it was.

It was immediately apparent how much more powerful and manoeuvrable it was when compared to the Blenheim. A strange innovation was the duplicated flying controls in the gunner's cockpit, a stick and a rudder bar, but no instruments nor could the gunner see where he was steering if he had to take control . . . Boston IIIAs had twice the power, carried twice the bomb load, but had only half the duration of the Blenheim.'

Boston crews flew many memorable day-

light attacks over France and the Low Countries from 1941-44, even being used as smoke-screen operators during the June 1944 invasion of Europe. Further afield, Bostons of the RAF and SAAF played a significant part in the 1942-43 operations in the Middle East.

Douglas Boston A Boston from 88 Squadron, Second Tactical Air Force, lays down a smoke-screen to protect the Allied invasion forces as they land on *Arromanches* beach on D-Day (6 June 1944). This version is a three-seater bomber, but there were also two-seater fighters and reconnaissance aircraft.

North American Mustang

Designed and developed from the outset for use by the RAF, the Mustang was the first-ever fighter produced by its parent company, North American Aviation. Initially fitted with an American Allison engine, the first Mustangs to be tested by the RAF proved disappointing for high altitude combat and were thus allotted to army co-operation roles, or tactical reconnaissance (Tac-R) as these duties came to be known. In this form a number of squadrons continued flying Mustangs in the Tac-R role until early 1945. The general opinion of the

North American Mustang A Mustang from 168 Squadron takes off on a reconnaissance mission from an advance airstrip in Normandy in summer 1944. This variant was fitted with the Allison engine, the long-range fighter-escorts had the more powerful Rolls-Royce Merlin engine.

Mustang with the Allison engine was that it was an excellent aeroplane, docile in control, with several outstanding features, but that it lacked sufficient surge in engine power. In late 1942, therefore, trials were flown of a Mustang fitted with a Packard-built Rolls-Royce Merlin engine. These showed that the Merlin-Mustang was more difficult to control, but was unquestionably superior in all combat facets.

127

Within a year Merlin-engined Mustangs were operational with the USAAF based in Britain, fitted with extra fuel tankage, and acting as 'Little Brother' escorts for the American daylight bombers ranging over Germany. With more modifications and constantly increasing range potential, the Merlin-Mustangs became the undisputed finest operational fighter of its period. Mustangs next operated in the Mediterranean and Far East, while several years later the design was again operational with the USAF and RAAF in the opening phases of the Korean war.

Jesse Thompson of the USAAF said of the P-51D (Mustang), 'There is no doubt in my mind that, on the whole, it was the best single-seater to see action in the European theatre.'

Squadron Leader F E Dymond RAF (Retd) recalls the Mustang:

In the latter half of 1944 I was stationed at North Weald as a member of 234 Squadron, one of the few operational units still flying the Spitfire Vb. In the September we were re-equipped, not as anticipated with the Spitfire Mark IX but with the Mustang III. It was a very pleasant aircraft to handle and although American-built we felt at home in it immediately, perhaps because of its Merlin engine.

In December we moved to Bentwaters where by early 1945 there were six squadrons of Mustangs. Our primary role was to provide long range escort to Bomber Command on daylight raids over Germany.

The recommended climbing speed for a fully loaded Mustang carrying drop tanks was 180 mph however when we climbed as a Wing of 36 aircraft it was easier to maintain formation by flying at 200 mph and climbing at 500 feet per minute. This slow climb was acceptable as our rendezvous point with the bomber force was not until we crossed the Dutch coast.

The aircraft was not designed as an interceptor but as a long range fighter and time to altitude was not a vital factor. With its large fuel-carrying capacity the Mustang gave us a range of action

that we had never enjoyed with the Spitfire. In the latter one always had an eye on the fuel gauge but in the Mustang there were no such worries. Not surprising really, with a maximum tankage of 349 gallons and a consumption rate of around 40 gallons per hour when cruising on weak mixture. Although I never flew there, Berlin was well within its reach with a margin for combat if necessary. It was a fighter with a terrific radius of action and practically viceless. Visability from the cockpit was excellent thanks to the Malcolm canopy which was a British innovation and far superior to the original type fitted to the Mark III (P.51B&C). Another

refinement was aileron trim control, hitherto unheard-of in single engined fighters but a welcomed feature on long sorties. As already stated it handled well and was a very stable weapons platform for its four 0.5 in guns, and the other armament stores it could carry.

The Mustang was originally designed to meet British requirements and when it was eventually married to the Rolls Royce Merlin engine I would not argue with those who claim it to have been the best Allied all-round fighter aircraft of the war, although some of our British fighters excelled in certain respects.

Douglas Dakota

Any record of transport aircraft of the world over the past 40 years cannot fail to pay tribute to the Dakota, the doyen of such aeroplanes. A military descendant of the DC3 airliner, the 'Dak' came into RAF use from April 1941 – the first 12 Daks going to 31 Squadron in India whose prodigious supply record throughout the Far East campaigns has few if any peers. Dakotas, of every type, continued in RAF frontline service, though in diminishing numbers, until the ultimate RAF Dakota (KN645) was officially 'retired' on 1 April 1970. Almost 11,000 Dakotas were eventually built, of which some 2000 were used by the RAF as the premier workhorse for supply and transportation in literally every battle zone of World War Two.

Every pilot who ever flew Dakotas developed a lasting affection for them, remembering their docility yet enduring toughness and stoic patience. Their feelings may possibly be summed by one ex-Dak skipper who once wrote, 'Having notched up over 8000 hours on the Dak I have nothing but affection and admiration for the old kite, and I can think of no other aircraft that could have taken the punishment that Daks received weatheriwise in SEAC (South-East Asia Command). For instance, I've had landing lamp glasses smashed by hailstones, wing rivets pulled, and the webbing straps that held the stretchers in position broken in turbulence – and still the old

lady flew on.' Or as one anonymous scribe once put it:
They patched her up with masking tape, with paper clips and strings
And still she flies, she never dies, Methuselah with wings.

Robert Pearson, one-time Warrant Officer, RAF, in 437, 271 and 215 Dakota Squadrons:
In wartime everything is a lottery. With flying training in South Africa completed, a toss of a coin decided whether I or somebody else should go to a squadron in the Middle East, carrying out shipping strikes in the Med. For me it was back to the U.K., to life on a Dak squadron – first as a second pilot, then as an aircraft captain – and a love affair with what must surely be one of the most remarkable aeroplanes of all time.

So what, apart from its technical excellence, so endeared the Dak to its crews and to everyone in uniform in war zones around the world? To pilots it was a thoroughbred, combining tenacity with impeccable manners – a delight to fly, forgiving and indomitable. One soon got used to what, in those days, seemed its large size – the cockpit some 20 feet off the ground with the aircraft at rest, the 95 feet wing span and those two marvellously reliable 1200 hp Pratt and Whitney Twin Wasp engines. For the soldier wounded in battle it was the lifeline to salvation, however remote the location. For anybody else with the need or the wit to win a

seat, it was an aerial bus to and from all kinds of
exotic and improbable destinations.

Even now, when occasionally a Dak passes
overhead, those sweet-sounding engines open the
floodgates of memory. The comradeship, the endless
toing and froing. The daily flights, in the winter of
1944-45, from our Gloucestershire base to forward
airstrips in Holland with anything urgently needed
which would pass through the wide double doors.
The often atrocious weather of that winter; the low
cloud, the mist, rain and snow and the need, come
what may, to keep to the air corridors in sensitive
areas. The pain of walking through a plane loaded
with grievously wounded soldiers, their stretchers
secured in tiers for the trip back to a British
hospital. The one bemused soldier I so well recall

Douglas Dakota A Douglas Dakota serving
with South-East Asia Command embarks a
reluctant mule on a rain-soaked airstrip in
Burma, while a second Dakota comes into land.

who, within the space of a few hours, had been in
action, wounded, captured by the Germans, liberated
by our forces and put on the plane. But above all
one remembers the humour and repartee of service
life, and the joy of flying a delightful, responsive
aeroplane.

Then the short detachment to the Middle East
with the foray down to Asmara, Eritrea's high-
altitude capital, with a night stop at Wadi Halfa in
the Sudan and the runway there dancing up and
down on the approach like a demented dervish in the

appalling afternoon heat. The air-lifting of marines to newly liberated Athens and the delivery of a plane load of bank notes to Patras on the other side of the country. The return to Cairo and, by stages, through North Africa and southern France to base and the Continental milk-runs again.

On 24 March, 1945, most memorable of days, the airborne crossing of the Rhine at Wesel by the British 6th and American 17th Divisions – a 200-mile stream of tugs and gliders (1305) and transports with paratroopers (1795). With a glider in tow the final stages were like a slow approach to Dante's Inferno. Dust, gun flashes, columns of oily smoke, burning aircraft and paratroopers and glider troops going down into battle while we turned for home.

Then crewing up for the Far East, the sudden end of the war and a brief interlude in Burma before moving down to Kallang Airport, Singapore. Troops still to be supplied in the continuing hostilities in Java; flights to Sumatra, Burma, Thailand, French Indo-China (present-day Vietnam) and Hong Kong, that last-mentioned a nice challenge with its airport having a sizeable hill backed by mountains not far from one end of the not over-long runway, the sea at the other (now it extends into the bay). But things like that the Dak took in its stride. As we used boastfully to say, you could land it on a sixpence.

Memories are still keen, too, of the cumulo-nimbus thunderstorms which built up every afternoon around Malaya and the Indonesian islands. These could tear a plane apart with their vicious up and down currents, as I found almost to my cost getting into Java one day. They sometimes stretched from horizon to horizon and from near sea level to heights greatly in excess of the 22,000 feet service ceiling of the Dak. It was not such a day, thankfully, when Lady Mountbatten, then in the Wrens, turned up with her brigadier escort for the three-and-a-half hour flight from Batavia (now Jakarta) to Singapore, a flight shared with piled-up mail bags and an assortment of passengers. How graciously she accepted our offer of rather stale sandwiches.

It was a colleague, however, who on one occasion had an admiral among his passengers on a flight to somewhere in China which necessitated at one stage some rather low flying over the Pearl River between Hong Kong and Canton. This august personage was on his return flight next day. As my colleague passed him to reach the flight deck a voice said, 'Tell me, are we flying or sailing today?' Life was like that then. Oh, happy days!

Hawker Typhoon

Entering service from July 1941, the Typhoon, or 'Tiffy' quickly acquired a reputation among the squadrons as a jinx aircraft. It had yet to resolve its teething troubles with its unproven Sabre engine, while other minor aspects of actual performance gave few pilots confidence in going to war in this 'seven-ton brute'. Due in no small measure to the persistent faith in the design by Roland Beamont, who had helped in test development, however, the Typhoon slowly came to be recognised as a magnificent low-level attacker, packing a lethal punch of four 20 mm cannons, with a turn of speed which completely outpaced any German fighter. Above all, perhaps, was the extreme toughness of the design, both in construction and in appearance. Though initially intended as a high altitude interceptor in the defensive role, the Typhoon's true *metier* was as a low-level offensive fighter, where its near-400 mph speed and solid stability in control augured well for its future. By 1944 Typhoons were being fitted with underwing rails for rocket projectiles and carriers for bombs – veritable flying arsenals, which were used to deadly effect in the first months of the Allies' invasion of Europe that year.

As one ex-609 Squadron member described the 'Tiffy', 'It was used initially to tackle low-flying Fw 190 hit-and-run raiders pecking around the south-east coast. Our Typhoons overtook these 190s like bats out of hell and

Hawker Typhoon A ground crew takes a respite while in the distance a Typhoon undergoes maintenance. This was an overwhelmingly effective ground-attack fighter that destroyed numerous German tanks in the summer of 1944.

then blew them out of the sky with the four 20 mm cannons. The snag was that our lousy Sabre engines could be very temperamental – and engine failure at nearly 380 mph at less than 200 feet altitude was hardly a laughing matter. It was an everpresent nagging worry to the pilots, but we just pressed on and trusted our ground crews.'

Avro Lancaster Path Finder

By mid-1942 the Lancaster was in full production and beginning to replace the outmoded pre-1939 designed bombers in the ranks of Bomber Command. In August 1942 a new specialised bomber formation came into being – the Path Finder Force (PFF) – equipped initially with four squadrons of mixed types of aircraft, with 83 Squadron as the only Lancaster unit of this founder-members' quartet. The PFF was to act as the spearhead for future night raids over Germany, providing accurate marking of the target for a following main force to destroy, and ensuring the highest degree of navigation to and from any objective. PFF air crews were, with rare exceptions, already veterans of the bombing offensive before transferring to the force. By 1944 the PFF was equipped solely with Lancasters for the heavy bomber role, plus Mosquitos for pin-point marking and bombing support in the PFF tasks. A measure of the hazards voluntarily undertaken by the crews of the PFF during its three years' war was the final tally of casualties suffered – a total of 3727 air crew members killed, or the rough equivalent of the air crew strength of 20 Lancaster squadrons, representing a sixth of Bomber Command's overall casualty figures for the whole war.

Wing Commander Anderson has described the problems of pinpoint bombing at night:

Bombing an area from twenty thousand feet is one thing. Attacking a small factory or a vital marshalling yard tucked away in the middle of a French town is quite another. So a method of very careful target control was introduced and the Master-bomber came into his own. Markers were dropped as before, but no bombs were dropped until these markers had been checked and if necessary corrected by further target indicators. Crews were then told exactly where to aim. So now it was possible to follow the whole progress of a raid from an operation room in England, and to hear the Master-bomber calling from somewhere in the Paris area, 'Hallo, Main Force, hallo Main

Avro Lancaster Path Finder Air crew at dispersal points make final preparations before climbing aboard their Lancasters. The height of this very large plane can be clearly seen – it stood over twenty feet off the ground – as can the two 0.303 Browning machine-guns in the nose turret.

Force, overshoot the yellows by two seconds'. And if smoke covered the markers or it was too hazy to see, the boys would be told to go home. Then they would have to jettison a few bombs just off the French coast as the loads were far too heavy for happy landings! It is believed one night that a very clever German tried to send our boys home by pretending to be a Master-bomber. Unfortunately we had omitted to give him the code-word!

Supermarine Spitfire PR XIX

The value of photographic reconnaissance (PR) was recognised at the outbreak of World War Two by a dedicated handful of RAF men, and specially modified Spitfires for this role were used from late 1939. Usually unarmed, lightened, and relying solely on sheer speed and altitude to evade interception, various PR variants of Spitfires were then operated throughout the war in most theatres. Last of the PR Spitfire variants produced was the PR XIX,

Supermarine Spitfire PR XIX A Spitfire PR XIX flies high above the Mediterranean on a photo-reconnaissance mission in 1945.

the sole Griffon-engined version to be employed on such duties. Like many other Spitfire marks, the XIX was something of a hybrid, combining a late Mark XIV airframe with a Vc wing, adding extra fuel tankage and provision for camera installations. Developed in 1944, the XIX could achieve 450 mph at 26,000 feet, and the bulk of XIXs built incorporated a pressurised cockpit. Longest-lived of all PR Spitfires, the XIX had been produced particularly with the needs of the India/Burma war in mind, and it was somewhat appropriate that the final operational sortie by any RAF Spitfire was flown by a XIX from Seletar, Singapore in April 1954. However, Spitfire XIXs continued in civil use as meteorological observers for a further three years in Britain.

Short Stirling

'The most expensive contraption ever invented for the purpose of lifting an undercarriage into the air'—such was the view of one of the earliest operational captains of the huge Stirling bomber; other less kindly thoughts were expressed by some crews as they ran the gauntlet of anti-aircraft barrages due to the design's lack of a safe operating altitude on bombing operations. The massive Stirling will always be remembered as the RAF's first four-engined monoplane bomber of 1939-45, but the issue of the first example of 7 Squadron in August 1940 was merely the beginning of a long period of frustration and technical snags which delayed the operational use of this new behemoth. Tentative sorties by a handful of Stirlings began in February 1941 but the bomber only began fairly regular operations from April that year. It was to remain in firstline service until 1945, though by late 1943 the Stirling had been retired from bombing sorties, and was thereafter much modified to act as a glider-tug, airborne trooper and general transport machine. Of the 1759 Stirlings built as bombers, roughly one-third were lost in action.

H R Graham (later Air Vice-Marshal) who commanded 7 Squadron in 1941, said of the aircraft, 'The Stirling, as originally produced, was a first rate aeroplane. However, it was not an easy aircraft to handle near the ground. The exceptionally long undercarriage gave it a steep ground angle and made a dangerous weathercock swing likely if you were not quick on the throttles.' The true cause of the Stirling's disappointing operational performance lay in higher authority's insistence on overloading the original machine by almost a third more than its intended all-up loaded weight; thereby making every take-off a marginal operation, and inevitably producing a crop of aerodrome accidents. The design with such unplanned overweight always failed to attain a safe operating altitude, thus inviting fighter attack and anti-aircraft fire. As in the case of so many other RAF aircraft, any successes achieved by the Stirling can mainly be attributed to the undaunted courage of its crews.

D Murray Peden, QC, DFC flew one of the first of the four-engined bombers:

The Stirling was a four-engined 'heavy' from the outset. Unfortunately, the Air Ministry

stipulated that the wingspan of the new bomber
must be less than 100 feet. It thus came in at one
inch over 99 feet. This archaic criterion stemmed
from a fact no more compelling than that the doors
on the standard RAF hangars were only 100 feet
wide. It posed near-insoluble problems. It meant,
for all practical purposes, that a fully loaded
Stirling would do its bombing around the 12,000
feet mark, an altitude well within the range of even
light flak, many varieties of which could be hosed
up in streams. Even this was often achieved only at
the cost of an extra climb on the last leg into the
target. With her four Hercules XVIs, a Mark III
Stirling burned roughly 500 gallons per hour under
climbing revs and boost; and on long trips every
pilot was acutely conscious of those figures, and of

Short Stirling Short Stirling IV glider-tugs
of 620 Squadron cross the Rhine on 24 March
1945, moments before releasing the Sixth
Airborne Division in their attendant Horsa
gliders. This Mark had four Bristol Hercules
XVI engines capable of giving 1650 hp.

how an extra climb would critically erode his fuel
reserve.

On the bombing run itself, those endless minutes
suspended over the glare of the target, the strain of
searchlights, flak, and fighters, was augmented for
Stirling crews by the knowledge that, thousands of
feet directly above them, bomb aimers in Lancasters
and Halifaxes had opened gaping bomb bays and
were already raining down bombs by the thousand.

One strove to concentrate on the flaming target indicators far below, and on the tense note of one's own bomb aimer's voice in the headphones calling course corrections for the run-up. But ignoring the peril did not dispel it.

An offsetting advantage was the Stirling's manoeuvrability – it had to be experienced to be believed. In the early career of the Stirlings, in 1941 and 1942, they had been employed on a considerable number of daylight operations against targets in Germany and elsewhere, during which they naturally came under fierce attack from German fighters. The Stirlings had acquitted themselves well. Not only did their agility make them difficult targets; but even with their standard .303 armament they shot down a number of their attackers.

Hawker Tempest

The Tempest was basically a refined Typhoon – a 'Tiffy with the bugs ironed out' – and, indeed, was tentatively labelled Typhoon II in its original conception in 1940-41. A much thinner semi-elliptical shaped wing, plus more pleasing outlines to the fin and rudder marked the obvious external differences, and an uprated Sabre engine all helped the Tempest V under factory test to achieve a top speed in level flight of 472 mph – faster than the contemporary official world speed record. Roland Beamont, 'champion' of the parent Typhoon, also flew Tempests and his first impressions were highly enthusiastic, 'In the Tempest we had a direct successor to the Typhoon with most of the criticised aspects of the latter either eliminated, or much improved. Each flight brought greater enjoyment of and confidence in the crisp ailerons, firm though responsive elevator, good directional stability and damping giving high

Hawker Tempest A Hawker Tempest V from 3 Squadron, flown by Flight Lieutenant Pierre Clostermann, engages in a dog-fight with Focke-Wulf 152s in April 1945. The Tempest was a radically-modified version of the Typhoon (see page 131).

promise of superior gun-aiming capability, exhilarating performance and, with all this, magnificent combat vision, with windscreen forward frame members thinned down to a bare minimum, and superb unobstructed vision aft of the windscreen arch through a fully transparent sliding canopy.'

The first Tempest Wing formed in April 1944 and they first saw action two days after D-Day. That same month, June 1944, brought the UK-based Tempests into combat with the German V1 'buzz-bombs' as these began their robot assault on southern England, and Tempests eventually destroyed 632 of them. The final months of the European war brought the Tempests into daily support tasks: ground-strafing enemy airfield locations, railways, roads, or other opportunity targets. Air opposition was sporadic but fierce, and included many clashes with Messerschmitt Me 262 jet fighters. Tempests remained in RAF squadron service until 1951.

Pierre Clostermann, DSO, DFC describes a dogfight in the Tempest (another is illustrated overleaf):

I spotted a lone plane skimming over the tree tops in the direction of Bremen, whose tall chimney stacks looked positively medieval outlined against the dying sky.

We were now over Bremen, and he was still about a thousand yards ahead. This business might take me rather far; I closed the radiator again and opened the throttle flat out. My Grand Charles responded at once. We were now over the first docks on the Weser.

Suddenly a salvo of flak shells blossomed between

the Focke-Wulf and me – brief white flashes, mingled with brown balls which passed by on either side of me. More kept appearing miraculously out of the void. The automatic flak now chimed in and the orange glow of the tracer was reflected in the black oily water, from which overturned hulks emerged, like enormous stranded whales.

I concentrated on not losing sight of my Focke-Wulf – luckily he was silhouetted against the dying glow in the sky.

For a moment the flak redoubled in intensity then suddenly the tracers were snuffed out and disappeared. A bit suspicious! A glare behind me explained this curious phenomenon: on my tail were six Focke-Wulfs in perfect close echelon formation – exhausts white hot – pursuing me at full throttle.

With one movement I broke the metal thread to enable me to go to 'emergency', and shoved the throttle lever right forward. It was the first time I had occasion to use it on a Tempest. The effect was extraordinary and immediate. The aircraft literally bounded forward with a roar like a furnace under pressure. Within a few seconds I was doing 490 mph by the air speed indicator and I simultaneously caught up my quarry and left my pursuers standing.

I had soon reduced the distance to less than 200 yards. Although in this darkness my gun might rather dazzle me, I had him plumb in the middle and I fired two long, deliberate bursts. The Focke-Wulf oscillated and crashed on its belly in a marshy field, throwing up a shower of mud. He miraculously did not overturn. Without losing any time I climbed vertically towards the clouds and righted myself to face the others. They had vanished in the shadows. They must have turned about and left their comrade to his fate.

Gloster Meteor

The Meteor, or 'Meatbox', was the RAF's first jet fighter, and indeed the only Allied jet aircraft to see operational service during World War Two. Its planning was undertaken in 1940 (before the revolutionary Gloster E.28/39 Pioneer single-engined jet had been built) but the first Meteor to actually fly (DG202) made

its initial flight tests in March 1943. In July 1944 the first two that were operationally fit arrived at Culmhead to begin re-equipment of 616 Squadron – Britain's first jet fighter unit. Moving to Manston, 616 Squadron commenced Meteor operations in July 1944, acting as interceptors against the V1 flying bombs, and

eventually claimed 13 of these. During the last weeks of the war a handful of Meteors were stationed in Europe, but these saw no aerial combat. In successively improved versions, the Meteor was destined to remain the premier firstline aerial defender of Britain for some 12 years, while certain squadrons saw long service in Germany and in the Middle East. Many hundreds of Meteors were bought by foreign air forces in the post-1945 years, though none was ever required to fire its cannons in anger, except those used by 77 Squadron of the RAAF which saw combat during the Korean War. During its long life the Meteor was subjected to a myriad of trials and experiments: in-flight refuelling, long-distance flights, high speed

Gloster Meteor A Gloster Meteor F3 of 616 Squadron intercepts a V1 flying bomb over the Home Counties in 1944. This the RAF's first jet aircraft to enter service was more primitive than the Me 262, its German counterpart.

reconnaissance techniques, ejection seat trials, prone position pilot cockpits, radar tests. In particular however, there were high speed record attempts. Meteor F4s were selected in 1945 for the RAF High Speed Flight, and Group Captain H J Wilson, DFC achieved 606 mph. The following year saw more attempts to raise Wilson's record speed, and this was accomplished by Group Captain E M Donaldson with a recorded 616 mph.

Aircrew run to board their Valiant during a Quick Reaction Alert

The Beginning of the Jet Age

As in 1918, the end of the war in 1945 saw the RAF again suffer from drastic reduction not only in numerical strength but in financial provision, resulting in several years' delay in converting its firstline equipment from piston-engined designs to jet-powered successors. For the first six years of the 'peace' Bomber Command's squadrons continued to fly piston-engined Lincoln and Washington bombers, but in 1951 came the first Canberra jet-bomber squadron in service; while Fighter Command added DH Vampires to its Meteor units in defence of the United Kingdom. Overseas squadrons, traditionally last in priority for new aircraft, plodded on operationally with piston-engined types, such as the Brigand and DH Hornet, until the mid-1950s; while Coastal Command had to be content with variants of the four-engined Shackleton—itself a development of the wartime Lancaster bomber.

From 1955 new muscle was added to the RAF when the first of a trio of jet-engined heavy bombers, the Valiant, joined Bomber Command, followed later by the Victor and delta-winged Vulcan—a combination of nuclear-age bombers which were to comprise Britain's nuclear deterrent force until 1969. In the fighter field came the superlative Hawker Hunter, followed in 1956 by the Gloster Javelin interceptor, but it was to be a further five years before the RAF received its first truly transonic fighter, the magnificent Lightning. As the latter entered service, RAF Transport Command commenced up-dating its potential with jet-powered DH Comets.

Avro York

In many people's minds the lumbering York is most associated with the immediate post-1945 era of RAF history, yet the aeroplane was conceived and first built in early 1942 and was a direct descendant of the mighty Lancaster from which it initially took its wings and tail unit. These were 'attached' to a much deeper, wider fuselage having roughly double the cubic capacity of its forebear, and the first York progressed from original drawings to the first prototype flight in a mere five months. Due to the contemporary Anglo-American agreement that all wartime transport aircraft were to be manufactured in the USA, the York was produced in small numbers at first, and several of the initial batches were immediately converted internally for VIP accommodation to ferry high-ranking politicians and Service chiefs, and on occasion royalty. Thus it was not until

Avro York One of 51 Squadron's Avro Yorks, taking part in the Berlin Airlift in 1948, runs up its engines at Gatow airfield before returning to West Germany for more supplies.

1945 that the first wholly-equipped York unit came into being when 551 Squadron received its full complement of the type. The York's RAF heyday came in the late 1940s when it came into special prominence during the Berlin Airlift. In this *Operation Plainfare*, Yorks alone flew some 29,000 sorties and lifted nearly a quarter of a million tons of supplies, apart from being mainly responsible for the carriage of civilians – virtually half the RAF's total effort during this prolonged operation. Of a total of 257 Yorks eventually produced, 208 were delivered to the RAF, and the last of these in service (MW295) remained in RAF livery until 1957 when it was sold to a Middle East civilian airline. Though by no means as tractable to fly as its 'parent', the York was a patient packhorse which eventually accumulated a prodigious amount of vital, if mundane, flying miles.

Wing Commander Cyril Povey flew Avro Yorks for more than four years and took part in the Berlin Airlift:

I went on to Yorks early in 1946 when I was transferred to 246 Squadron at Holmesley South near Christchurch. Our main task was to bring back from the Middle East and Far East people who were due for demob and take out replacements. I thought the York was a lovely aeroplane by the standards of those days. It was docile, pretty steady to fly and had no nasty vices. The engines were very reliable; in perhaps a couple of thousand hours of flying Yorks over a period of four years I had only one engine failure in the air, which is pretty good going. The York was not as beautiful an aeroplane to fly as, for example, the Mosquito and the Beaufighter. In fact, it was a lumbering heap as all transport aircraft were, but as transports went it was a good aircraft. It was a much nicer aeroplane to fly than the Handley Page Hastings was, for example, although the Hastings was a more modern aircraft. I think all the York's virtues, especially its reliability, were shown to perfection in the Berlin Airlift.

When the Berlin Airlift began in 1948, 246 Squadron went to Wünnsdorf near Hanover, which until then had been the base of some Vampire fighter squadrons. Then the whole place became a transportation set-up. The operation was very, very well organised from the start with improvements constantly being made.

Our Yorks mainly carried foodstuffs such as grain, tinned foods, sacks of sugar, powdered milk, egg substitute and so on. All the seats had been taken out leaving the long fuselage completely empty and when we took off we were always crammed full of cargo. The few passengers we did carry were either very senior or were serious medical cases being flown out of Berlin for better treatment elsewhere. We would fly three return trips to Berlin a day, which took fourteen hours (the average flight time was about an hour) round the clock.

Aircraft were constantly taking off and landing at the Berlin airfields, making the air extremely crowded. For that reason the very best air traffic controllers were there and that makes a tremendous difference, but you still could have only one stab at a landing. If you misjudged it, you just carried on in the pattern and took the load home to base. Normally, when you missed an approach you could circle around and try again but not over Berlin – the sky was much too crowded, and any such action would very likely have brought you directly into another stream of oncoming aircraft. Bringing a load back was always embarrassing, but of course an inexperienced pilot would fly as a co-pilot to gain experience.

The Russians attempted to harass aircraft in several ways. At Gatow there were Russian anti-aircraft guns just off the end of the runway which would fire practice rounds at all sorts of odd times, and we were never quite sure when we took off whether they were going to start firing at us or not. That was uncomfortable, much more so than being 'buzzed' by fighter aircraft while flying to and from Berlin.

We assumed that they weren't going to fire on us and so it wasn't terribly worrying to see them there. An aeroplane is not a very frightening thing unless it starts shooting at you! By the time the Airlift ended in May 1949, we had proved that it was possible to keep a large city supplied from the air, although there was an enormous amount of belt-tightening. I don't think the Communists ever imagined that we could do it but we did.

De Havilland Hornet

The aesthetically-appealing Hornet was not only the RAF's last piston-engined fighter to enter squadron service, but was also the fastest of its type and class. Patently derived from the huge success of the all-wood Mosquito, the Hornet was nevertheless an entirely new design. Its conception was as a long-range interceptor, capable of matching any Japanese fighter, for use in the final stages of the Pacific campaigns. Great attention was paid to reducing cross-sectional area in fuselage and engines in order to enhance speed, and basic armament com-prised a four 20 mm cannon battery in its slender belly. Planned and built in 1942-43, the prototype Hornet first flew in July 1944 and immediately exceeded its expected perform-ance figures, reaching a maximum speed of 485

De Havilland Hornet A pair of F Mark 3 Hornets from 41 Squadron soon after take-off. They are painted in the camouflage worn by long-range intruder aircraft of the period.

mph. The first production Hornet reached the RAF in February 1945, but it was not until March 1946 that the first fully-equipped squadron was declared operational, this being 64 Squadron based at Horsham St Faiths (now Norwich Airport). Only three other UK-based squadrons were Hornet-equipped thereafter, and these became Meteor jet fighter units by 1951. That year saw the Hornet finally move to the Far East, when three other squadrons in Singapore and Malaya received Hornets, and flew these almost daily on operations against Chinese communist 'bandits' in the prolonged *Operation Firedog* until in turn being replaced by jets from 1955. In Malaya the Hornet's cannons were supplemented by underwing rockets and carriers for up to 2000 lb of bombs. A fully navalised version, the Sea Hornet, was also built in reasonable numbers, but equipped only two squadrons fully; while the final variant was the PR Mark 22 – a high-speed photo-reconnaissance machine which saw limited use.

Avro Lincoln

Designated originally the Lancaster IV or V (according to type of engines fitted), the Lincoln was built to a 1943 specification and intended for use in the Pacific war against Japan. First flown in June 1944, Lincolns were first issued to 44 and 57 Squadrons late in 1945, and eventually equipped 20 RAF squadrons. The design was historically significant as being the final piston-engined heavy bomber to see RAF squadron use, though some were replaced temporarily by Boeing B-29 Washingtons for a brief period. The aircraft's extended range and bomb load capacity – 14,000 lb at maximum storage – led to a variety of active operations in the various post-1945 uprisings and rebellions in overseas zones; notably during the Malayan Emergency and the anti-Mau Mau campaign in Kenya. In these periods, UK-based Lincoln squadrons were detached for one or two months in rotation to appropriate RAF bases overseas. The Lincoln's high altitude performance also saw the type employed in a wide variety of purely aeronautical experiments. Batches of Lincolns were bought by Australia and Argentina for normal bomber roles, while individual examples undertook a number of very long distance flights in the interests of research.

Finally withdrawn from RAF firstline use by 1963, the bulky Lincoln – its wings spanned 120 feet – was not a particularly easy bomber to like. It handled reasonably well and performed its duties doggedly, but as one Lincoln pilot put it, 'The sheer size of this black beast was frightening at first acquaintance, but the most vivid memory of several years in a Lincoln's driving seat was the noise inside the cabin. After four or more hours up front in a Lincoln, my hearing was semi-defective for hours afterwards.'

Avro Lincoln The Avro Lincolns of 7 Squadron on a bombing mission against Malayan terrorists in 1954. This aircraft was a development of the Lancaster, but its improvements included a greater wing-span, improved engines with four-blade propellers and a longer fuselage.

Bristol Brigand

The Brigand's main operational contribution, between 1950 and 1954, was as a light bomber or, more usually, a ground-attack strike aircraft. Its original conception in 1942, however, had been as a torpedo-bomber replacement for the Beaufighter which was temporarily fulfilling such a role with Coastal Command at that time. The prototype Brigand first flew in December 1944 and owed much to its stablemate the Buckingham bomber design, and although initial deliveries to the RAF were torpedo aircraft, these were soon converted for the pure bombing and strike role and then reallocated to units based in the Middle and Far East commands. Indeed, the Brigand, which was another development of the Beaufighter (page 105) served in a wide range of environments that were unsuitable for aeroplanes such as the wooden Mosquito. In Malaya Brigands served briefly with 45 Squadron before being replaced by de Havilland Hornets, while those allotted to 84 Squadron at Tengah continued anti-'bandit' strike sorties until as late as 1953, when—resulting from a number of fatal crashes due to structural reasons—84 Squadron was 'disbanded' in situ and its Brigands reduced to scrap on site. Thereafter the only Brigands in service were flown as radar navigation trainers on UK-based OCUs until early 1958 when they were finally withdrawn from service.

An ex-signaller with 84 Squadron remembers the Brigand as, '. . . a noisy, sweaty aircraft in which to operate. The perspex glasshouse for the crew was like a sauna bath when one climbed in for a strike sortie from Tengah. Operating at jungle-height was never comfortable, while the

wings always appeared to be ready to part company with us every time we went into a rocket attack dive. My pilot usually referred to the kite as "the black bastard" . . . I shared his opinion'.

Bristol Brigand Two Brigands from 84 Squadron let loose a salvo of rockets at a terrorist position in Malaya in 1952. The Brigand had been developed from the Beaufighter (page 105), but was radically adapted into a three-seat ground-attacker.

De Havilland Vampire

A contemporary of the Gloster Meteor, the de Havilland Vampire jet fighter was designed in 1941 but did not reach RAF squadron service until 1946. For the following five years Vampires established a high reputation for their aerobatic qualities and formation flying displays in Europe and abroad. Though generally superseded in Fighter Command by the Meteor by 1951, the Vampire created many firsts in RAF history. Six aircraft of 54 Squadron made the first RAF jet crossing of the Atlantic in July 1948; it was the first jet fighter to see service in both the Middle East and Far East areas; it was also the first jet aircraft to be issued to units of the Royal Auxiliary Air Force. And in December 1945 a navalised Sea Vampire became the first pure jet ever to operate from an aircraft carrier. From 1950 to 1954 the only Vampires to fire their cannons in anger were those equipping two squadrons of the Far East Air Force (FEAF) based in Singapore and Hong Kong, which flew numerous sorties in the Malayan anti-'bandit' campaign.

Always popular with its pilots, the Vampire (along with the Meteor) was equally popular with its ground maintenance crews – a relatively rare attribute. Its compact design and easy access for servicing, re-arming and refuelling,

enhanced its reputation among the ever-toiling 'erks' – one of whom has described the Vampire as '. . . the neatest little jet fighter ever invented, even if it did suffer from ducks' disease!'

De Havilland Vampire Vampires of 501 (County of Gloucester) Squadron, Royal Auxiliary Air Force between sorties during summer camp at Odiham in 1949. This single-seater jet fighter was powered by a Goblin turbojet engine rated at 3100 lb of thrust and had a maximum speed of 540 mph.

Blackburn Beverley

A military version of the intended civil transport GAL Universal Freighter of 1946 genesis, the Beverley came into RAF service from March 1956, when 47 Squadron began the change-over from the unit's Hastings aircraft. At that time the lumbering Beverley was the largest aircraft ever seen in RAF livery, and its design and general configuration incorporated no few innovations for its designated role as a freight and troop carrier. The rear-loading doors – then unique in RAF experience – permitted easy access for a wide variety of loads; while the aircraft's remarkably short take-off and landing runs enabled the gentle giant to operate to and from bald desert airstrips at will. Only five squadrons were equipped with Beverleys and a mere total of 47 machines were actually

Blackburn Beverley A Beverley on a desert airstrip in Aden while another circles overhead. This transport aircraft was the largest aeroplane to be seen in RAF service up to that time yet it could take off and land in a surprisingly short distance.

produced for the RAF; yet these gave some 12 years' faithful, virtually trouble-free operational service before finally being retired in 1968. During those years Beverleys saw active operations in several trouble-spots around the globe, particularly in Aden, Kenya and during the brief Kuwait 'oil crisis', while in early 1966 three of 47 Squadron's amiable mammoths were 'detached' for 18 months to Da Nang Air Base in Vietnam to assist in lifting relief supplies to the interior of that war-ravaged country. Others flew over the Malaysian jungles from Singapore bases, and some participated in the Brunei uprising.

Avro Anson

'Faithful Annie' was the universal and affectionate nickname for one of the RAF's hardest-working and long-lived aircraft. Just as its ancestor the Avro 504 had 'taught a nation to fly', so the Anson carried on the tradition by providing basic airborne instruction for a later generation of air crews. Entering service with 48 Squadron in March 1936 as a coastal reconnaissance aircaft, the Anson was the first RAF aeroplane to incorporate a retractable undercarriage in firstline use. At the outbreak of World War Two a total of 301 Ansons were with Coastal Command – representing exactly two-thirds of the command's aircraft strength. By the close of 1941, however, all Ansons had been replaced at squadron level, and the design reverted to what proved to be its greatest contribution to the RAF – as a training or communications machine. Chosen as a standard instructional aircraft for the Commonwealth Air Training Plan, the Anson trained many hundreds of bomber crew members; while in its 'hack' transport role, the Annie flew with most RAF units and in particular the Air Transport Auxiliary. More than 11,000 machines were built, and the Anson was officially retired from RAF service in June 1968 – the close of 22 years of faithful service.

The Anson's reputation among experienced pilots was once summed succinctly by an ATA pilot, 'It is virtually as easy to fly as a Tiger Moth, and just about as viceless. In fact, a pilot would really have to try to kill his passengers in an Anson which is just one of the many good reasons why it is such a good machine. Others are its ease of maintenance and extreme economy, its astonishing reliability, and the fantastic loads it will carry. Added to all of which it can be flown in and out of the tiniest aerodromes . . . Undoubtedly the Anson is one of the most wonderful aeroplanes that has ever been built.'

H A Taylor flew the Anson many times:

Myths are built up around nearly every aeroplane. For the Anson the myth was one of reliability and harmlessness. Annie, the Old Lady of Woodford, could never, never turn and bite you; her Cheetah engines never stopped; and any fool could handle her.

In fact, the Anson could, like any other aeroplane ever built, turn and bite; the Cheetahs did sometimes (though very rarely) stop before the cutout wire had been pulled; and it was not particularly easy to fly. But it was a forgiving old thing.

The interminable windings for undercarriage retraction were an acceptable agony and the work kept pilots and pseudo-crews in better physical condition than they might otherwise have enjoyed. The sliding fuel cocks to the right of the second

pilot's seat will be forgiven even by those who lost so much skin when operating them from the driver's seat on the other side of the aisle. Ground (and some flight) crews may even remember, with no more vicious reaction than a nostalgic shrug of the shoulders, their struggles with the engine-starting handles.

Those of us who lived with the Anson as a taxi hack from day to day will not forget, either, the desperate feeling of helpless frustration when the brake-operating pressure in the ground-filled air bottles began to fail when we were turning on to the runway for a last, late evening trip. And if the throttles were carelessly handled at the beginning of the take-off the Anson could, like any other twin, dash in a humiliatingly uncontrollable semi-circle.

Avro Anson An Avro Anson T21 serving with No 18 Reserve Flying School on a training flight in 1952. By that date the aircraft had been in service for sixteen years and had undergone numerous modifications; it would continue in service for another sixteen years before being finally retired in 1968.

The 'book' said that it would not remain continuously airborne when flying on one engine – but a test pilot friend of mine flew one successfully on the starboard engine from somewhere north of Worcester to RAF Aston Down on the top of the Cotswolds. When safely overhead this aerodrome he gained as much height as he could, using override power on the good engine. Then he spun the

undercarriage crank through its scores of turns and made a conventional pre-1940 dead-stick approach—complete with S-turns, sideslips and all the rest of it. He had been brought up in the era when all landings were forced landings and in an environment where it was nothing less than shameful to drag an aeroplane in on the engine(s) at tree-top height.

For some of us the Anson had special memories. It was the aeroplane into which the ferry pilot tumbled thankfully after the last delivery flight during a sometimes harrowing day. It was, for many RAF maintenance units, the communications hack; a test pilot at one of these units breathed a sigh of relief when the day's programme required him to do no more, perhaps, than to make, with the Anson, a round of equipment-collecting visits to other units and factories.

Of course, the Anson was sometimes treated too carelessly by people who had not yet learned that all aeroplanes are, by the nature of the laws of Sir Isaac Newton, intrinsically dangerous.

Once, while making a final approach in an Anson, I noticed some surprising and variable changes in the fore-and-aft trim. The landing was completed without incident, but I was surprised that my test-pilot passengers were so insistent that there would be no need to put in a report to the unit's chief technical officer. It transpired that these over-healthy young men—on a test-flying 'rest' between operational tours—had been 'playing harps' with the bare wires running through the fuselage.

For me, there is one reason why the Anson is an exclusive aeroplane. In it I learned to fly with my left hand while doing all kinds of other things with the one which had been originally taught most of the tricks.

Gloster Meteor F8

Though many different marks of Meteor served with the RAF at various periods, probably the best-known was the Mark 8, which from 1950 to 1956 was the main single-seat day fighter of the UK-based RAF. The F8 was in essence a much-improved F4, with longer fuselage, uprated engines, and a modified cockpit to accept a better-vision canopy and an ejector seat. Armament remained the same, but all-round performance was noticeably improved, giving the F.8 a top speed nudging the 600 mph mark. The Meteor F8 was gradually replaced on the firstline squadrons from 1956 onwards, but the type lingered for several more years as a target tug. The F8 was the only 'peacetime' Meteor to see active service in the

Korean war, when 77 Squadron RAAF exchanged their Mustang fighters for Meteor F8s in early 1951. Actual war operations by the Australians began in late July and continued until the end of the war in July 1953.

Squadron Leader Bill Waterton, DFC, GM, Gloster's chief test pilot, flew many of the various marks of Meteor:

The prototype Meteor 8 was smooth and pleasant to handle. It was faster than the Mark 4 despite its extra weight – 15,200 lb against 14,700 lb. During trials I reckoned it was doing 605 mph at 5000 feet, and I put this down to the cleaning-up of airflow over the improved tail. While the Mark 4 pitched and bucked when approaching the speed of

Gloster Meteor F8 Three Gloster Meteor F8s of 601 Squadron, Royal Auxilliary Air Force, practise aerobatics while on a summer camp in Malta. The most obvious difference to the earlier Meteor (see page 140) was its redesigned tail and cockpit.

sound, the very first 8 simply showed slight trim changes and dropped a wing. It was lighter to manoeuvre and an easier spinner. Its ailerons were still heavy, however, and remained so until new spring-tabs were introduced. In production however Mark 8s did not repeat the prototype's pleasant characteristics . . .

Supermarine Swift

Significant as the RAF's first-ever swept-wing fighter in operational squadron use, nevertheless the Swift's only true claim to fame came in September 1953, when Lt-Cdr Mike Lithgow established a new world speed record of 737 mph in a specially-prepared Swift. The Swift was produced as a 'safeguard' high altitude interceptor in case the Hawker Hunter, then being built, proved to be disappointing in service. In the event it was the Swift which was

Supermarine Swift A Supermarine Swift FR5, operated by 79 Squadron in Germany from 1959 to 1961, on a low-level sortie.

considered a somewhat dismal failure for its intended role. A host of modifications and trials failed to give the design the essential attributes of a firstline defender, and its later variants were accordingly converted to low-level high-speed tactical reconnaissance machines. In squadron use the early marks were underarmed – just two 30 mm cannons and assorted rocketry at best – while the aeroplane's undesirable longitudinal control characteristics and engine deficiencies condemned it for the particular needs of the UK-based Fighter Command. Based in Germany, just two squadrons were equipped with the later fighter-recce (FR) version of the Swift and these performed satisfactorily in their tasks. This FR version was the first RAF jet in squadron service to incorporate a re-heat engine capability, and remained in service from 1956 to 1961.

Handley Page Hastings

Superseding the Avro York as the RAF's standard long-haul transport aeroplane, the Hastings served with RAF squadrons from 1948 until the type's official retirement in 1968. Almost immediately after reaching its first squadron, the Hastings was in action – participating in the latter stages of the Berlin Airlift. During its 20 years service the Hastings served the RAF magnificently. Like all 'willing workhorses' in the RAF's history, it undertook an astonishingly wide variety of tasks: freighter, paratroop conveyor, meteorological surveyor, ambulance, VIP luxury transporter, radar bombing trainer, navigational instructor, heavy cargo lifter – these and other minor roles were

Handley Page Hastings Hastings from 511 Squadron, Transport Command, drop the parachutists of the Third Battalion, Parachute Regiment over Port Said during the 1956 Suez Crisis. The Hastings was the RAF's standard transport plane for over a decade.

all grist to the Hastings' mill. Nor were these roles always carried out in peaceful skies. Apart from the emergency measures of *Operation Plainfare*, the capacious Hastings saw active service during the Malayan Emergency (*Operation Firedog*), the Korean War, and, in 1956, in the Suez Crisis (*Operation Musketeer*). The demise of the Hastings was eventually due simply to fatigue – literal fatigue of its air-frame components; but by the time of its withdrawal from RAF squadron use, the type had flown more than 150 million miles, and 'lifted' some one and a half million passengers and nearly 200,000 tons of freight over virtually every part of the globe. Its splendid service history fittingly continued its parent firm's long tradition of providing dependable 'heavies' for the RAF which had begun in essence with the Handley Page 0/100 biplane behemoth of 1914-15.

De Havilland Chipmunk

Designed and built by De Havilland's Canadian company, the tandem two-seat Chipmunk was a direct successor to the firm's Tiger Moth for *ab initio* training in the RAF. As elementary instruction aircraft, Chipmunks were used from 1950 to 1973 in sporadic phases – depending on whatever contemporary fashion in flying instruction was in vogue with the RAF – and were considered to be delightfully easy aeroplanes to operate, with good handling characteristics and a high degree of aerobatic capability in the hands of an experienced pilot. Able to operate comfortably from even small grass airfields, Chipmunks provided a first taste of

flying for many thousands of RAFVR (Royal Air Force Volunteer Reserve) and National Service pilots, apart from regular RAF personnel, and was the type chosen for the initial flying instruction undertaken by HRH the Duke of Edinburgh in 1952.

De Havilland Chipmunk A trainee pilot puts a de Havilland Chipmunk through its paces. This two-seater trainer was a direct successor to the same firm's Tiger Moth (page 100). The Chipmunk was in use as an RAF trainer from 1950 to 1973.

Vickers-Armstrong Valiant

The Valiant, as Britain's first operational four-jet bomber, exemplified RAF Bomber Command's true transition from the piston-engined force of the 1940s to the nuclear deterrent bomber strategy of the 1950s and onward. It also gave practical 'birth' to the

RAF's V-bomber force created to implement that fresh strategic policy. Entering squadron service in April 1955 – two years before its compatriots the Avro Vulcan and the Handley Page Victor – the Valiant was the only V-bomber to release bombs in anger when it flew operations in the Suez Crisis; while in 1956 and 1957 Valiants were responsible for dropping Britain's first atom bomb and hydrogen bomb respectively during nuclear trials in the Pacific. It remained in squadron service for almost ten years, during which period reconnaissance and in-flight refuelling tanker variants were also introduced. In the latter role the Valiant extended the RAF's flexibility in striking power globally, and a number of successful inter-continental long-range flights by various Valiant crews emphasised this versatility. Despite the seeming complexity of such a radically new concept of bomber, the Valiant was found to be relatively easy to service and maintain, while its handling qualities were considered generally good by its air crews. Official disbandment of the Valiant V-force was announced in February 1965, due to a number of metal fatigue defects discovered in main wing spars, and the design swiftly faded from the RAF scene. Nevertheless, the Valiant had spearheaded the RAF's entry into the 'nuclear club' and its pioneering experience was the foundation for Britain's future strategic policies in bombing operations.

Chief Technician Fred Flower served as a crew chief with 18 and 49 Squadron for several years:

With the introduction of the V-bombers, of which the Valiant was the first, the RAF decided that it would need an aircraft servicing chief on American lines, and in consequence many senior NCO airframe and engine fitters had to do a pretty concentrated crew chief's course involving the maintenance of the airframe, engines, electrics, and a fair knowledge of the radar and wireless equipment fitted. The course was about nine months and was very concentrated – too concentrated, especially if you weren't from Bomber Command to start with. The Valiant introduced the complexities of electricity on a large scale, as most of the major operating procedures – flap operation, airbrakes, undercarriage retraction etc. – called for electrical power where they would normally have been hydraulic.

In the case of the Valiant the only hydraulics were the nose-wheel steering, and even there the hydraulic power was brought in by electrically-controlled hydraulic pumps. (Except, of course, for the self-contained Powered Flying Control Units.)

As crew chief, you were in charge of the servicing, and in theory, wherever the aeroplane went, you went with it. This sometimes involved what were called 'lone rangers', overseas postings where you flew with the aeroplane, with no-one at all to help with the maintenance except the air crew you were with. The ideal thing was for a crew chief to be assigned to one aeroplane, and to stay with it; though obviously if someone went on leave or was sick, you ended up looking after more than one aeroplane.

From the crew chief's point of view, the bad thing about the Valiant was that there was no provision made actually to carry the crew chief. The result was that you could go off on a four-, five- or six-hour flight with two pilots in very comfortable seats, who could eject out if necessary, with three rear crew members in reasonably comfortable seats and a crew chief who either squatted on the floor or stood up all the time hanging on to the handgrips. They did attempt to rectify the situation a few months before the Valiants were finally grounded, but even that would have involved sitting on the floor in between two of the rear crew members. Even so, one felt proud to be associated with the squadron, and felt important going off on these lone rangers; there is no doubt that you were treated with some respect.

What impressed me when I joined 49 Squadron (Marham) was the degree of operational readiness. It wasn't like a peacetime air force; as far as I was concerned when I went on to V-bombers the country might just as well have been at war. The aircraft on QRA (Quick Reaction Alert) were all bombed-up, ready to go, and it was a case of maintaining every aeroplane in a thoroughly serviceable state. They might even want an engine changed, and you had to press on straight away and get the defects cured, as the aircraft was probably wanted the next day and there had to be some pretty good reasons if it wasn't serviceable to meet that requirement.

I later joined 18 Squadron whose Valiants were not operated in the bomber role as this was an RCM (Radio Counter Measures) Squadron. This necessitated aerials being mounted along one bomb

bay door and that door being rendered inoperable. Ideally, in a squadron of only seven aircraft, you would have one plane on a major inspection, and at least five of the other six standing on the aerodrome serviceable.

It says a lot for the Valiant that we could cope with that requirement, but I have horrible memories of changing fuel tanks with the temperature way below zero; the fuel tanks were rubber cells and the cold did nothing to make the rubber flexible. Given a warm hangar, then even the job of changing fuel tanks was considerably eased, but a lot of the servicing had to be done outside and it was nothing unusual to see engine changes going on outside.

Vickers-Armstrong Valiant A Vickers-Armstrong Valiant B1 of 148 Squadron lands at Luqa, Malta after a mission to Egypt during the 1956 Suez Crisis. It remained in service for almost a decade and fulfilled a number of different roles.

163

Hawker Siddeley Javelin

The largest fighter ever adopted by the RAF up to that time, and the world's first delta-winged operational aircraft, the Javelin owed its basic shape, in part, to the results of studies undertaken by a few German scientists for the Luftwaffe and subsequently analysed by RAE Farnborough shortly after the close of World War Two. Its initial trial and test programmes resulted in the deaths of two test pilots and illustrated several serious handling and flying defects, but steady modification and improvement in the light of experience allowed the Javelin to be introduced to RAF squadrons from February 1956, two years after the Hunter's operational debut. Compared to the Hunter, the Javelin's all-round performance was inferior, but its accommodation for extra

Hawker Siddeley Javelin A Javelin FAW 7 from 23 Squadron takes off from a rain-soaked runway at RAF Coltishall, Norfolk in 1959. This was the RAF's first delta-wing fighter and was also the first designed to fly in any weather and at night.

radar and other black box equipment made it highly suitable for night interception roles. At least nine distinct Marks of Javelin were built, but the initial Mark Is issued to the RAF were considered by many pilots to have been the best version for squadron use. It was generally thought of as a pilot's aeroplane, with all-vital equipment and controls close to hand, easy to operate, and simple to check. Cockpits were thought to be well-designed, comfortable to use, while handling was considered excellent. Its greatest fault – common to most marks of Javelin – was its poor stall recovery characteristics; normal recovery in a Mark I being almost impossible and, in part, responsible for several aircraft and crew losses in operational use.

Bill Waterton, who flew in many of the Javelin prototypes' test trials and was awarded a George Medal for bringing back a Javelin which had shed its elevators due to excessive flutter, said of the aircraft, 'The Javelin was easy to fly, had an excellent performance and showed great promise. She had some dangerous tendencies too, such as reversing her longitudinal control (the stick had to be pushed instead of pulled) near the stall, tightening into the turn, and pitching strongly nose-up when the flaps were extended.'

Westland Belvedere

Helicopters, now very much part of the everyday aviation scene, were not used operationally by the RAF until 1945, and even then merely by introducing British-built American designs. The efficacy of the 'chopper' for frontline tactical use became well evident in the Malayan Emergency operations, apart from its widespread use by the USAF in the Korean War; hence British interest was stimulated in several aircraft firms. Westland's twin-engined, twin-rotor Belvedere – the first of its class in RAF service – entered squadron usage in late 1961, and was designed to fill several support roles, including trooping, freight supply, and casualty evacuation for ground forces. Capable of lifting some 6000 lb – internally or externally – Belvederes saw widespread action during their eight years' RAF service, operating in Europe, Aden, Africa and in the Far East during the 1962-66 Brunei campaign. Though designed for one-engine reliability if required, the Belvedere's all-round performance was never outstanding, and its squadron crews were never entirely enthusiastic about the type; indeed, several crashes at Aden in 1965 brought the design into dubious repute for a time.

Wing Commander J R Dowling, MRE, DFC, AFC has had wide experience of the Belvedere. He not only formed the initial Belvedere Trials Unit but also later commanded a helicopter Wing in Borneo which included the Belvederes of 66 Squadron:

The Belvedere had a number of firsts to its credit. It was the first helicopter specifically ordered to provide tactical support for the Army; it was the first twin rotor helicopter and the first turbine-engine helicopter to come into RAF service.

Basically, the Belvedere was two Sycamore helicopters joined together, back to back. Its twin rotor design meant that it did not have the centre-of-gravity problems that are bound to affect a single rotor helicopter, since such a configuration ensures that there is no residual torque to be corrected and produces a further advantage in that the aircraft is not sensitive to wind direction when it is hovering. In other words, the Belvedere could hover as efficiently cross-wind as into the wind, unlike a tail-rotor helicopter.

Prior to the Belvedere, helicopters had been limited in what they could lift by the power available from the engine, and the pilot had to be wary of the load of the aircraft in relation to the amount of power available at that particular attitude and temperature. If he miscalculated he was in danger of over-pitching. But the turbine engines of the Belvedere supplied more power than could be used. Indeed, in British conditions they were rarely used at more than half power – a pilot could lose one engine and still fly at the same performance.

Production models of the Belvedere appeared in late 1961 at which point development stopped for financial and other reasons. In fact, the Belvederes which were put into service were described by the designer as mere operational models. Certain mistakes were made, the most tiresome of which

---

Westland Belvedere A Bristol Belvedere of 26 Squadron, based in Aden, lifts a 105 mm howitzer into position for J Battery, Royal Horse Artillery, during the Radfan Operations in South Arabia in 1964. This was both the first twin rotor helicopter and the first turbine-engine helicopter to enter service in the RAF.

concerned the starting system whose unreliability was a major problem. There were also other technical problems, most seriously with those operating in Aden, but in general the aircraft was eminently satisfactory from a flying point of view.

Unfortunately, the Belvedere had a comparatively short lifetime. There was no hard and fast strategic case for having helicopters of that size in long-range support to the Army and short-range support could be adequately dealt with by first the Whirlwind and then the Wessex. Now the RAF has Chinook helicopters, which the Belvedere resembled in many ways. I think the Belvedere came too soon; it was too early for its own good.

Hawker Siddeley Hunter

The elegant Hunter endeared itself to all who were privileged to fly it. In the words of the distinguished fighter pilot Peter Wykeham, 'The slim fuselage, thin swept-back wings, tailplane and fin, and the delicate balance and

Hawker Siddeley Hunter A Hawker Hunter FGA9 from 20 Squadron, the Far East Air Force, flies past a native settlement in Borneo in the mid-1960s. The Hunter was a superbly versatile combat machine that could be a fighter, bomber or reconnaissance aircraft.

proportion of the whole aircraft were the very poetry of motion.' Anyone fortunate enough to have witnessed the breathtaking formation aerobatics of 111 Squadron's 'Black Arrows' in the 1950s, or 92 Squadron's 'Blue Diamonds' in the early 1960s could only agree with that description. As the RAF's first supersonic operational fighter, the Hunter initially equipped 43 Squadron in 1954, and became Fighter Command's standard single-seat fighter until being gradually replaced by the English Electric Lightning from 1960 in Britain. Later marks of Hunter continued in frontline service overseas until 1971, playing a major active role in operations in the Middle East and Far East.

Neville Duke, the wartime fighter pilot who had much to do with the development flying of the original Hunters, has put on record his thoughts, 'For me there is no greater satisfaction than sitting in the cockpit of the Hunter, beautiful in design and construction, representing the thought and skill of so many people, and feeling it respond to the slightest movement of your fingers. It lives and is obedient to your slightest wish.' From a Service viewpoint, an ex-8 Squadron Hunter pilot once remarked, 'When I arrived on the squadron I had some years of fighter experience behind me, but after only one sortie in a Hunter I felt I'd never *really* flown a fighter before. Its touch was perfect, control a real enjoyment, and manoeuvrability a wonder. I've flown more modern fighters since, but none compare with the superb Hunter.'

Westland Whirlwind Helicopter

The patent success and versatility of the American Sikorsky S-55 helicopter led to its adaptation by the RAF from 1953, retitled as the Westland-built Whirlwind. It also entered service with the Royal Navy, and in progressively modified and improved forms remains in service still. Its duties have been widely varied: jungle rescue and evacuation, air-sea rescue, communications, troop transport, VIP transport, emergency medical transportation, and a dozen other roles. The early versions were fitted with piston engines, but replacement of these with turbine powerplants lengthened the

useful life of the aeroplane, and added reliability and greater range to its performance. Whirlwinds saw operational service with the RAF during the Borneo confrontation of the 1960s, adding the supply role to its ubiquitous tally of duties; and, in several cases, being converted for use as a gun or missile carrier for low-level strafing sorties. Apart from its purely military or naval roles, it is a familiar sight to the civil population around Britain's coastline, and in its rescue role has saved the lives of several thousands of holiday-makers and maritime crews in distress.

Flight Lieutenant D P Holmyard is a navigator who has flown in the Westland Whirlwind on numerous Search and Rescue missions, including those with 21 Squadron at RAF Manston:

The Whirlwind has a crew of three : pilot navigator/winch-operator and winch-man. Its radius of action is 90 miles, allowing it to undertake inshore and coastal missions while the Sea King helicopters perform the longer missions.

The outstanding feature of the helicopter is its

Westland Whirlwind Helicopter A Whirlwind HAR 10 from D Flight, 22 Squadron based at Manston, Kent on Search and Rescue Duties picks up a survivor from a stricken yacht. The winchman is lowered by the navigator who also calls out guidance to the pilot.

precision and manoeuvrability in calm conditions, it can be steered to hover within merely a few inches of movement; that is everything you could want from a machine that needs to do precision winching such as

170

is necessary when picking up an injured person from a ship with a lot of rigging lines or from a cliff with a large overhang. In such a situation the navigator/winch-operator acts as the pilot's eyes, directing him upwards and downwards, backwards and forwards, to the left and right. The winch-man is lowered, he comes off the winch-hook to look after the injured person while the Whirlwind holds off, then reconnects himself and the injured person to be pulled up and taken back to shore.

The Whirlwind is currently being phased out of Search and Rescue Operations. In time, instead, there will be flights of Sea King helicopters and Wessex helicopters dotted around the UK in overlapping circles.

Hawker Siddeley Gnat

The Folland-designed Gnat fighter was never adopted by the RAF in its intended role, but its conversion to a two-seat advanced jet trainer was accepted by the service, and the latter version began its service with the CFS in early 1962. Capable of becoming supersonic in a shallow dive, the nimble Gnat offered all the necessary handling and flying characteristics of the modern jet interceptor to its pupil crews, and was fully aerobatic at low or high altitudes. This latter quality has never been better exemplified than its many public performances with the CFS's formation team, the Red Arrows of the 1970s. Flown in superlative style by instructors from the CFS, the Arrows brought the art of formation aerobatics to the peak of perfection, thrilling millions of spectators all over Europe. Considering its power – an ability to reach Mach 0.97 in level flight – yet astonishing manoeuvrability and instant, positive control, it is seldom realised just how relatively small the plane is. Its wings span a mere 24 feet, while overall length extends to just 31 feet and 9 inches. It stands a mere 10 feet 6 inches off the ground at its maximum height, making it a very compact aeroplane indeed.

When one considers the multi-million pounds' cost of producing a present-day single-seat military jet aircraft, the sheer economy in costs, materials and labour-hours needed to to produce a true lightweight, operational interceptor or strike aeroplane—the Gnat's original conception—is still perhaps worthy of attention. Its arrival on the military scene was, perhaps, ill-starred, coming into being at a period of governmental retrenchment in military expenditure.

Hawker Siddeley Gnat Gnats of the RAF Red Arrows aerobatic team, led by Squadron Leader Ray Hanna, perform at the 1968 Royal Revue at Abingdon. This highly manoeuvrable aircraft entered service in 1954 and for more than two decades it was the RAF's standard advanced jet trainer.

Avro Shackleton

Planned initially as the Lincoln Mark III for anti-submarine attack roles, the Shackleton was originally designed to replace the long-range lend-lease Boeing Fortresses and Consolidated Liberators of Coastal Command at the end of World War Two.

With the gradual phasing out of its Sunderland flying boats in the 1950s, Coastal Command relied heavily upon the Shackleton for its prime maritime reconnaissance duties, and in gradually improved versions, the Shackleton was to remain in squadron use until the early 1970s. In 1957 the MR3 variant began to replace older variants in service, thereby introducing the now-familiar tricycle under-carriage to the type. As an airborne 'antidote' to submarines, the Shackleton could lift a multi-varied warload, having provision in its bomb bay for bombs, depth charges, etc.

Avro Shackleton An 8 Squadron AEW (Airborne Early Warning) 2 Shackleton passes over Gibraltar, on detachment from RAF Kinloss. The Shackleton has been operational from 1951 to the present day.

Jaguar single-seat fighters as seen from the cockpit of a Jaguar two-seat trainer

The Royal Air Force Today

A succession of misguided changes and decisions of governmental policy throughout the 1960s and 1970s robbed the RAF of such superb concepts as the TSR2 strategic bomber, but from 1969 – when responsibility for Britain's 'nuclear deterrent' was transferred to the Royal Navy's *Polaris*-armed submarine fleet – the RAF was reshaped as a future tactical support force. As such it began to receive USA-designed Phantoms and the revolutionary British Harrier VTOL aircraft, while the remaining V-bombers were converted into low-level attack bombers or air tankers for in-flight refuelling tasks.

From 1975 Phantoms began replacing Lightnings as UK-based interceptors, and the Anglo-French joint-designed Sepecat Jaguar was designated to succeed the Phantom in its former ground assault role. Today, the vast expense of producing any form of military aircraft almost enforces production of designs capable of fulfilling every major role – a concept exemplified by the latest addition to RAF strength, the Panavia MRCA (Multi-Role Combat Aircraft) Tornado. It will, in essence, replace existing aircraft individually tasked with fighter interception, overland strike, reconnaissance and maritime strike roles; and present forecasts indicate that Tornado aircraft will comprise almost 60% of RAF strike strength in the 1980s. In support will be some 200 Jaguars, and perhaps 40 jet-powered Nimrod anti-submarine 'hunters' for pure maritime duties.

BAC Jet Provost

The Hunting Percival Provost of the 1950s was the RAF's ultimate piston-engined standard basic trainer, and from it was developed the BAC Jet Provost in accordance with a contemporary training policy for 'all-through' jet aircraft instruction for embryo RAF pilots. The neat Jet Provost came into service from 1955 and its easy-to-handle characteristics quickly proved popular with instructors and pupils. Gradually improved and modified, later versions of the Jet Provost formed the equipment of several RAF aerobatic formation teams for public exhibitions and displays in the late 1950s and early 1960s. In late 1969 the latest variant, the T5, entered RAF service, having a pressurised cockpit and many of the most modern avionics incorporated. With its maximum speed well in excess of 400 mph, and an ability to operate above 35,000 feet, the T5 Jet Provost could thus accustom its crews to the demands of modern jet operations. HRH Prince Charles received his advanced flying instruction in a Jet Provost at RAF Cranwell, going solo after just eight hours' dual control.

Group Captain John Lacock has spent several years flying the Jet Provost, and training pilots on it:

Many of our trainee pilots come from the University Air Squadrons where they will have been flying piston-engined Bulldogs, but the Jet Provost has been used for basic pilot training since the early sixties and 'ab initio' pilots went straight on to them. Recently, though we have introduced a familiarisation scheme where students who haven't

BAC Jet Provost The instructors of No 1 Flying Training School, Linton-on-Ouse, Yorkshire indulge in mirror formation practice, 1969. RAF trainee pilots, if they have had no previous flying experience, need approximately 100 hours on the T 3As shown here to reach 'wings' standard, as well as another 60 hours on the Mark T 5A.

flown before do 20 or 25 hours in a Chipmunk to get air experience. The basic course is 150 hours, which takes about ten months to complete, before you go on to the advanced trainer Hawk.

In some ways the jet is an easier plane for young people to come on to than a piston-engined aircraft. When you apply take-off power to a piston engine plane, for instance, it tends to turn sideways and go off the runway, which can be quite difficult for a student to cope with initially. The jet pointing right down the centre line with the thrust light pointing straight forward goes straight down the runway rather than turning. Another problem with earlier trainers was the fuel-induced piston engines. These meant that there was an unpleasant smell that pervaded the cockpit, and the environment for the new student could be very upsetting. Many young people feel a certain amount of travel sickness when they get airborne for the first time and that was accentuated by the smell of gasoline fumes. There are none in the jet, and the Mark V has a pressurised

cabin, very similar to sitting in a sports car.

It is, like all good training planes, one that handles conventionally and doesn't spring surprises on the inexperienced pilot. The Mark V is relatively new and will probably be flying through the 1980s, or even longer, to make it a three-decade plane, which is reasonably good value.

When we get back to flying after a spell in a desk job, the first thing we do is have a refresher course in a Jet Provost, and it's something that we all thoroughly enjoy. Under the old system we used to keep all pilots in current flying practice by closing the office on certain days each month when we would go up; but that was a difficult system to work and made people thoroughly dangerous. Nowadays you are assigned to a squadron for six months at least, and the basic training is done on a Jet Provost to get your flying skills back to decent speeds before you go on to other planes. So as a result it's a plane we all feel a good deal of affection towards.

Lockheed Hercules

With the drastic reduction in Britain's overseas territories and commitments overseas following World War Two, the crucial need for mobility of the much-reduced RAF's potential striking force and of the army provided a much greater requirement for large, long-range aircraft

capable of transporting troops and supplies over vast distances at very short notice. Interim designs such as the Hastings and Beverley filled the medium range role in this context, followed by the Argosy in the 1950s and 1960s. To supplement these air carriers, the RAF pur-

chased a mini-fleet of the giant American Lockheed Hercules tactical transport – known to its USAF crews as the Herk or Herky-Bird. Able to lift almost 100 passengers and kit over ranges up to 4700 miles, the Hercules first joined 36 Squadron in August 1967 (11 years after its original acceptance by the USAF). Within a year, four more RAF squadrons were declared operational on the Hercules, including 48 Squadron based at Singapore. Powered by four Allison turbo-prop engines, a loaded Hercules could accomplish a cruising speed of nearly 370 mph. Despite its size – its wings spanned nearly 133 feet, and fuselage length was almost 100 feet – the Hercules was relatively simple to operate and handle.

Lockheed Hercules A Lockheed Hercules of 24 Squadron flies through an electrical storm over the Alps during a support mission to Austria in August 1971. A loaded Hercules had a cruising speed of approximately 370 mph and a range with maximum payload of over 2400 miles.

British Aerospace Lightning

On the introduction of the superb Lightning in 1960, RAF Fighter Command entered a new era, for the Lightning was its first true supersonic fighter. Capable of achieving a speed of Mach 2 in level flight (more than twice the speed of a Hunter), the Lightning was also the real beginning of defensive aircraft that had been designed from the outset as a complete weapons system; this was a radical change from the hitherto design philosophy of produc-

British Aerospace Lightning BAC Lightning interceptors of 11 Squadron tail chase through storm clouds over Lincolnshire in 1974. (For a closer view see page 184).

ing a fast fighter and then 'adding' its offensive armament. Designed initially by W E W Petter of the English Electric Company, the Lightning was a bold step into the future; in effect the company had undertaken the design and production of a transonic, operational fighter in a single stage, and the result was a superlative aircraft by any criterion. It was received with acclaim by its RAF pilots: handling was excellent–a pilot's aeroplane–and it packed the necessary punch and urge to tackle any other aircraft in existence then.

In June 1960 the first Lightning squadron, No. 74 'Tigers' at Coltishall, received their first examples of the new fighter, and were declared fully operational by early 1961. Thereafter the Lightning became the RAF's standard defensive fighter until well into the 1970s. And for the greater part of its long service the Lightning, in most of its many forms, lived up to the succinct opinion of Squadron Leader

J F G 'Swazi' Howe who, as commander of 74 Squadron in 1960-61, flew the first operational example, 'We know that we can catch any current bomber, and . . . we know that we can outfight any fighter. This knowledge that we have the finest interceptor in the world gives the pilots tremendous confidence.'

McDonnell Douglas F-4 Phantom

The RAF's enforced budget cuts of 1965 and 1968 cancelled orders for the British TSR2 and American F-111 strike aircraft intended to ultimately replace the ageing Javelins and NF Meteors in squadron use, and left the Lightning as the RAF's sole standard interceptor. Accord-

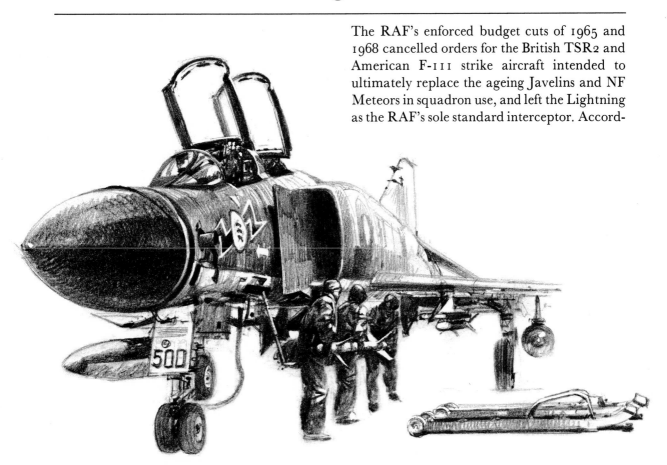

McDonnell Douglas F-4 Phantom A
Phantom of 43 Squadron, based at RAF
Leuchars, Fife gains height to shepherd a
Soviet Tu-20 Bear (top) high above the North
Sea.

ingly, a previous order for F-4 Phantoms for the
Royal Navy was supplemented by orders for
more F-4s for the RAF as interim replacements
until the Jaguar became available. The first
Phantom arrived in Britain in mid-1968 and
by the end of 1969 a total of 168 Phantoms had
been delivered for the RAF. Supersonic in
speed and capable of lifting up to eight tons of
modern offensive armament, the Phantom had
already been in use by American air services
since 1960, and its employment as a pure
fighter in the Vietnam conflict proved relatively successful, with USAF F-4 crews claiming a total of 108 MiG enemy jets shot down. In
RAF service the F-4 is used in two main forms:
as a defence interceptor, and as a low-level

attack and reconnaissance aircraft.

Lt-Cdr R Cunningham USN flew F-4s in
combat in Vietnam, being the first five-victory
ace in that war, 'The F-4 will almost "talk" to a
pilot. She will tell you every move she's going
to make . . . but is as forgiving as she is honest
and won't throw you into an uncontrollable
spin. The F-4 is good at fast speeds but also
handles well in the low-speed range. The MiG
17 was easily the best-turning of the Soviet-

built jets used in Vietnam and could turn at 19 degrees per second as against the rate of 11.5 degrees per second for the F-4. As for the MiG 21, the trick was to manoeuvre it down to (usually) below 20,000 feet; that's where the Phantom really performs well and will turn and accelerate well.'

Squadron Leader Graham Cullington on the Phantom:

The Phantom is a relatively easy aeroplane to fly, and indeed I believe that in the United States it is even being flown by National Guard pilots, who only fly it at weekends. It is a typically American plane in many respects; for instance, its cockpit is larger than you would usually find in a British-designed aeroplane and this undoubtedly helps the pilot's efficiency. Although the Phantom is a heavy aeroplane, and consequently less manoeuvrable than many others, what makes it a great air defence aeroplane is its excellent weapons capability. The Phantom's weapon load and radar performance undoubtedly make it one of the world's finest all-round combat aircraft.

British Aerospace (Handley Page) Victor

The last of the RAF's trio of V-bombers to fly, the graceful, crescent-winged Victor was incidentally the last Handley Page bomber to be ordered for the RAF. Deriving from the 1946-47 decision by the British government to develop the atomic bomb and a four-jet engined bomber force capable of delivering nuclear weapons, the first prototype Victor made its initial flight in December 1952. Prolonged trials and testing—including several crashes and crew deaths—resulted in the first operational squadron, No. 10 at Cottesmore, only receiving their first Victors from April 1958. As other units gradually began receiving Victors for the nuclear bomber role, develop-ment continued to produce Victors for other tasks; these were chiefly the strategical reconnaissance, or flying camera-ship, role and, by 1965, as in-flight refuelling tankers. From 1964 modified Victors began to be flown in a very low-level bomber role, while adaptability trials were carried out to marry the Victor to the Blue Steel missile. By the close of 1968, however, bomber versions of the aircraft were phased out of squadron service. This left only the high-speed tanker version to continue its vital contribution to the RAF's global flexibility and mobility in a role initially pioneered by Valiants of 214 Squadron, commanded then by Wing Commander M J Beetham (later ACM Sir Michael, Chief of Air Staff), but which from 1965 was taken over by Victors.

Squadron Leader A Kearney flew Victor tankers for several years. Here he discusses the process of refuelling both from the tanker's and the receiver's viewpoint:

The role of the Victor tanker has changed over the years. Its primary role a decade ago was that of strategic deployment: we would take people out to Singapore three or four times a year and we also did some work with the navy. In recent years, though, the emphasis has completely changed. Deployments are now a secondary feature, instead the primary role of the tanker in a tactical sense is to refuel the aeroplanes of UK air defence or maritime air defence.

The aim of the tanker pilot is to make a rendezvous, get on a tow line and give as much fuel as possible to the receiver. Most refuelling takes place at altitudes in the mid-twenties (such as at 25,000 feet) although some of the newer aircraft prefer to be lower at about 20,000 feet. The Lightning performed best in the mid-thirties, but that was exceptional; that altitude was good in terms of ordinary deployment but would be a little more vulnerable during hostilities. In close formation where one Victor is refuelling fighters, then the fighters must manoeuvre while the Victor maintains position. However, we regularly have three or four Victors in formation perhaps joining up with a flight of Phantoms, and for that situation the Victor pilots must be quite skilled in formation flying.

Refuelling is fairly simple for a tanker. It's a crew effort in terms of getting to the rendezvous and bringing the aircraft together, but once this has occurred it becomes a very passive manoeuvre from the tanker's point of view. Hoses are trained and the receiver comes in to make contact. The tankers do day and night refuelling, and the latter is probably the most demanding task for any pilot in the tanker force.

To refuel, the receiver has to fly in very close formation, which is quite difficult in a large aeroplane, get in very close into a stabilised position 8-20 feet behind the centre hose and make that final contact. In daytime there are visual cues; the markings that run across the wings are a help initially, and the pilot can see the hose and orientate himself to the aeroplane and to the horizon. At nightime most of the visual cues are gone. All that remain are the centre-line lighting where the hose leaves the aircraft and the hose itself. The procedure is carried out purely by sight and, because there is no visible horizon, there can be a mild sense of disorientation. In practical terms, if you are in current receiver practice, by day you should make contact within four attempts—I would say that at night this number is probably doubled.

British Aerospace (Handley Page) Victor

A Victor K2 Tanker from 57 Squadron extends its fuel hoses to refuel a Lightning of 5 Squadron. Lightnings normally refuelled at altitudes above 30,000 feet, which is significantly higher than more modern planes.

184

Michael Turner '81

Short Belfast

Only ten Belfasts were ever built for the RAF, but at the time of their entry to squadron service – with 53 Squadron at Brize Norton in January 1966 – they were the largest-ever aeroplanes to wear RAF livery, having wings of nearly 159 feet span and a length of fuselage stretching over 136 feet. They were also the largest aircraft in the world to be fitted with a fully operational automatic landing system. With an all-up weight of 225,000 lb (102,220 kg) the Belfast was certainly the heaviest RAF aircraft in squadron use, yet pilots reported its handling characteristics favourably; as one pilot put it, 'Once you got over the awesome feeling of being in control of a mobile block of flats, she responded normally to control, with no major problems.' The cathedral-like

Short Belfast A Short Belfast from 53 Squadron comes in to land with supplies for the British Defence Forces in Belize in 1975. Only ten Belfasts were ever built, and they operated all over the globe in the decade following their entry into service with the RAF in 1966.

spaciousness within the fuselage provided easy accommodation for loads of up to 70,000 lb-plus, or 150 fully-kitted troops or other passengers. Though few in number, the Belfasts accumulated many millions of miles of flying around the globe during their overall ten years RAF service, but after one of the periodic governmental cuts in defence budgeting all were gradually phased out of use by 1976. Its place as a long-range strategic freighter was then taken over by the Lockheed Hercules, which still performs this function.

British Aerospace (BAC) Canberra

The sleek and deceptively slim contours of the Canberra tend to hide the fact that besides being Britain's and the RAF's first jet bomber, it proved to be one of the most versatile and adaptable aircraft designs in the annals of aeronautical history. Designed to a 1945 Air Ministry specification, the prototype first flew in May 1949, and began to re-equip RAF squadrons from May 1951. With an internally-stowed bomb capacity for up to 6000 lb, and speeds well in excess of 500 mph, the Canberra inaugurated a new era in British bombers. Since that time the development potential of the basic design has been exemplified by a pro-liferation of variants: a ground attack, photo-reconnaissance, nightfighter, radar and ECM dual trainer, target tug, crewless 'drone', night interdiction – these are merely the major roles undertaken by Canberras over the years. Canberra crews became the first to operate jet bombers in the Far East, flying anti-terrorist bombing sorties in Malaya; while the Suez Crisis in 1956 saw Canberras used as strike bombers against Egyptian airfields and installations. Long-range overseas flights were undertaken without problems by various Canberra

formations during the early 1950s, and individual machines set up fresh speed records for such items as trans-Atlantic double flights. Bomber Canberras were finally phased out of firstline use by the end of 1961, but PR and night intruder versions remained in service until the early 1970s. In all, some 40 RAF squadrons have flown Canberras at some period of the design's outstanding life during which a grand total of 27 Marks of this long-lived and versatile aircraft were built.

British Aerospace (BAC) Canberra A Canberra PR7 of 13 Squadron, based in Malta, caries out an aerial survey of earthquake damage at Gemona, Northern Italy in May 1976. This, the first British jet bomber, began flying in 1949 and is still in as much use as ever.

Wing Commander Colin Adams has described the photo-reconnaissance work of the Canberra:

The Canberra PR7 was the backbone of the

photo-reconnaissance force, with squadrons in the UK, Germany, Malta, Cyprus and the Far East. But the plane really came into its own during the Borneo confrontation. The plane was originally designed for high-level reconnaissance with a set of six cameras for vertical work, but it could also do oblique and low-level work. Normally in the Canberra the navigator takes the pictures lying in the nose, where there is a sight for him. He has to be very accurate, particularly for mapping work where you have to get the photos overlapping to complete the picture. Some of the early versions had an extra navigator taking pictures out of the back of the plane, as the pilot cannot see behind him.

The surveying work was used for all sorts of purposes. Some squadrons were for reconnaissance on the battlefield, photographing troop movements and military installations. But I have done many other jobs too. In England I have done tasks for the Ministry of Housing and local government, surveying potential sites for new towns in West Sussex – which rather horrified me as I come from around there – and photographing the approach roads into London to work out traffic patterns and establish

where to put new roads. Often we would do a job for the local government when we've finished our military task. In Trinidad we were doing a survey of the island, and the government also asked us for some pictures of the harbour to help build a new harbour wall; and while I was doing a complete mapping survey of the New Hebrides there was a boat lost and I sent the Canberra out to find it. I've used the Canberra to photograph aircraft accidents and train crashes. Photo-reconnaissance is one of the most fascinating roles in the RAF, as a result; you visit a lot of interesting places and you can actually see what you have achieved.

The Canberra is now quite an old plane. Photo-reconnaissance has never had such an important role as it had in the Second World War; the Canberra was going to be replaced by the TSR2 before that was scrapped, and eventually the Tornado will have a reconnaissance role in addition to its other duties. Many of the surveying jobs can now be carried out rather better by satellite, which can give higher resolution pictures. But many countries can't afford to pay for a satellite survey, and if there is a Canberra there, they will still get us to do the surveys for them.

British Aerospace (Hawker Siddeley) Buccaneer

The rapid development of radar for detection of enemy aircraft – the prime ingredient of the RAF's struggle in 1940 and in the subsequent night operations over Britain and Germany – led logically to urgent consideration in the post-1945 RAF to aircraft capable of penetrat-

ing enemy territory under the existing radar defence systems. The Buccaneer was the first RAF aeroplane specifically designed for such a task – ultra low-level sorties deep into hostile countries to avoid any radar 'umbrella'. It was originally conceived for naval carrier operations and equipment of RN units commenced in 1961. In 1968, with the cancellation of contracts for re-equipping RAF squadrons with the swing-wing F-111, however, orders were placed for Buccaneers to fill the gap in the RAF's frontline units, and these began reaching RAF squadrons from late in 1969. At speeds approaching Mach 0.85, Buccaneers in their prime role usually fly at less than 200 feet altitude, literally hugging the terrain in any

British Aerospace (Hawker Siddeley) Buccaneer A Buccaneer S2B from 237 OCU, Honington builds up a condensation barrier on a fast, low-level run off the East Coast. The Buccaneer functions as both a low-level strike and reconnaissance aircraft.

attack approach. Actual flying, navigation and eventual target acquisition rely almost entirely on highly sophisticated black box instrumentation, radar, television guidance and predicted flying patterns for operations. The aircraft's structure is specially strengthened to withstand the inevitable buffetting, stresses and fatigue of 'grass-cutting' altitude flying; while low altitude manoeuvrability is reported as excellent.

British Aerospace (Hawker Siddeley) Nimrod

The menace of the submarine during the two major wars of this century with its power of virtually sealing off Britain from vital imports' lifelines by sea was self-evident. In the present era, with the submarine's added capacity to act as an underwater launching pad for nuclear-headed missiles, its potential threat is hugely greater. The RAF's foremost 'antidote' to the nuclear-armed submarine is the Nimrod – appropriately named after the mythical Hunter. The world's first four-fan jet long-range maritime patrol aircraft, the Nimrod was a direct development of the De Havilland Comet 4 and first flew in its original prototype form in 1967. In operational guise, it entered squadron service from 1970, and in its anti-submarine role carries the largest array of missile and

British Aerospace (Hawker Siddeley) Nimrod A Nimrod maritime reconnaissance aircraft, serving with 203 Squadron, takes a look at a Soviet destroyer in the Mediterranean. Nimrod was a mythical hero famed as a mighty hunter, which makes it an appropriate name.

detection and destruction equipment ever lifted by any RAF aircraft. The Nimrod's latest version is fully equipped as an Airborne Early Warning System (AEWS)–an aerial watchdog for early detection of any intercontinental missiles. With its overall range of some 6000 miles, and speeds approaching 600 mph, the Nimrod succeeds the Shackleton as Britain's prime maritime patrol and anti-submarine hunter; while its development potential and ability to incorporate all the latest forms of detection radar, computer, and/or offensive armament promises an active life for the Nimrod for the next two decades.

British Aerospace (Hawker Siddeley) Harrier

The conception of vertical flight ability is hardly new, but its application to the aeroplane in the military context was only truly exemplified successfully 20 years ago, when the Hawker P1127 first demonstrated vertical take-off and hover, or V/STOL as it was termed. Final development of the P1127 resulted in the Kestrel fighter–the first jet V/STOL aircraft put into RAF service. A supersonic development of the Kestrel was planned, then cancelled by governmental order, and instead a subsonic variant was progressed as a ground-attack fighter for the RAF, in the Harrier. Similar in appearance to the Kestrel, nevertheless the Harrier was virtually a completely new project with only some 5% of components common to both designs.

First to convert to the operational Harrier were the pilots of No. 1 Squadron RAF in June-July 1969, and initial reaction to this highly unorthodox fighter may be summed in the description given by one of those 1 Squadron pilots, 'The Harrier seemed at first sight to be almost deformed. Her squat bulbous fuselage crouched over a set of wheels like a broody hen on the nest . . . the whole aeroplane seen from afar when approaching to land strongly resembled some sort of flying ant . . . yet she breathed that undefinable sense of power. Her hunch-backed shape seemed to exude a threat to pounce on anyone foolish enough to walk by and ignore her. The cockpit was snug, and festooned in admirable logic with a multitude of miniature gauges, switches, lights and levers.' Apart from its upward take-off and hover capability, the Harrier handles well in the conventional performance envelope at up to near-Mach 1 speeds; while in its later forms it carries formidable armament, and adds a new dimension to tactical air warfare over land or at sea.

According to Air Vice Marshall Hine, who commanded the RAF Harrier Corps in

Germany in 1974-75:

The Harrier is virtually unique, as the only plane to combine the characteristics of the high-performance ground-attack jet with the capabilities of the helicopter. The particular advantage of this is that instead of being confined to a vulnerable main airfield, we have been able to develop the concept of the 'dispersed site operations', with only six or eight aircraft at each site, hidden in a wood. The plane can take off and land on fields of hard grass, or on

British Aerospace (Hawker Siddeley) Harrier A Harrier takes off from a dispersed site in winter. This was the first vertical take-off plane to enter service, which it did in 1969, and is certainly the forerunner of numerous similar aircraft.

two or three hundred metres of straight road. As well as the safety advantage, this can mean that the Harrier can be used well forward in support of

ground forces, maybe only ten minutes away from where operations are taking place, whereas the nearest airfield may be 25 minutes away. The result is you can do many more sorties in the course of a day than with a conventional aircraft; so that even if the Harrier does not carry as large a payload as a conventional plane, the number of weapons on target in a day can be higher.

There are a number of reasons why no other country has yet developed a V/STOL aircraft. The first is that many people think that the dispersed site operations are too complex logistically. That is not really true, especially if the site is within twenty miles or so of a main base; the equipment required to maintain a Harrier force in Germany for instance is considerably less than the Army requires for an armoured regiment. Another criticism is the Harrier's relatively short range and small weapon capacity. But that is not a criticism of the V/STOL concept itself, and the Harrier is very much a first-generation V/STOL plane. I'm sure that future designs will overcome these limitations, especially as the vertical take-off capacity is of much less

importance than the vertical landing, which is essential to get the plane hidden quickly. And perhaps another reason is the not-invented-here syndrome.

The bulk of the Harrier's flying is done at very low levels. You can get a pretty rough ride of course but it is a very safe plane. This is borne out by the fact that we teach people to fly a Harrier in all its modes in 21 sorties only, a total of 13 hours. It's extremely exhilarating to be flying at 250 feet at 550 knots one moment, and then, literally in the space of ten miles to slow down to the hover and land on a 50- or 70-foot square metal pad in the corner of a field and 30 seconds later to be inside the wood in a hide being turned round. The V/STOL capability gives the Harrier another unique feature, in its turning performance. Though in normal flight it is very similar to other conventional aircraft, you can vector the nozzles to increase your rate of turn, and alter the angle of attack in the aircraft in combat. You can literally make the Harrier turn a corner using thrust vector acting in a centripetal sense. This feature enables the Harrier to survive in *combat against the aircraft of an inherently much better performance. The real payoff comes at lower speeds when the conventional planes begin to run out of lift and the rate of turn falls off markedly, while*

you can move the Harrier about on its axis. And so you can bring guns to bear, even at very low speeds, wdich would be impossible for conventional aircraft.

British Aerospace (Avro) Vulcan

The doyen of the RAF's trio of V-bombers, the delta-wing Vulcan was ordered into quantity production before the first prototype had even flown. First to equip with the type was 83 Squadron in July 1957, followed by 101 Squadron in October of the same year. Third to receive Vulcans was the much-publicised 617 Squadron, in May 1958. The early B1 versions could carry a bomb load of 21,000 lb with ease, and general handling and maintenance was found to be surprisingly conventional considering the design's unconventional appearance. After some three years extensive RAF use on global flights and weapon-testing, the B1 was gradually superseded by the larger, better-powered B2 versions commencing in 1960. The B2 offered superior high-altitude performance and extended range (some 4600 miles without refuelling) and became the main vehicle for the 'stand-off' bomb/missile technique then being used by RAF Bomber Command, particularly

with the Blue Steel missile. From 1966 Vulcan B2s were further modified to undertake ground-hugging penetration roles, and three years later the Blue Steel partner was withdrawn, leaving the aircraft with conventional war loads. From the early 1970s Vulcans replaced Victors in the strategic reconnaissance (SR) role. Today the Vulcan is still very much a spine of the RAF's offensive strike armoury, despite its longevity in service, and will continue to be so until its eventual replacement by the Tornado.

Group Captain John Lacock on the Vulcan:

I first became involved with Vulcan operations in 1968 when stationed at Goose Bay in Labrador, and a year later joined 44 Squadron, Waddington, which also operates Vulcans. The aircraft is now firmly placed in the strike attack role and as such has the dual capability of carrying both conventional and nuclear weapons, and it also performs strategic, or maritime, reconnaissance duties at 27

British Aerospace (Avro) Vulcan A Vulcan B2 of 617 Squadron passes over the Fylingdales Early-Warning Radar Station in 1975. This is the only delta wing aircraft still operational.

Squadron. The wonderful thing about the aeroplane is that it was designed to operate as a high-altitude weapons system, but because of the improvements in surface-to-air systems in its lifetime it has been forced into use in the low-level role, which is a much more demanding physical regime for an aircraft, and has adapted to this role extremely successfully.

The mark of a 'thoroughbred' aeroplane, such as the Vulcan, is flexibility in the basic design that allows improvements to the performance of the various parts of the aircraft over the years, especially the engines and electronic systems. In the 1960s the Vulcan was re-equipped with uprated engines to allow the aeroplane to carry the weight of the forthcoming Skybolt missile, the successor to Blue Steel. The missile was cancelled, but the Vulcan crews have had the benefit for well over a decade of engines capable of producing much more power than the aircraft normally needs to carry out its basic role on the squadrons, which is an appreciable safety factor.

The Vulcan is definitely a 'pilot's aeroplane' – I have never yet encountered an RAF pilot who disliked flying it. It is possibly the most spectacular airframe as a display vehicle for the RAF that we have, and is certainly the only large delta wing aircraft to have stood the test of time as a display vehicle.

British Aerospace (Scottish Aviation) Bulldog

Originally designed and built by the now-defunct Beagle Aircraft company, whose first example made its initial flight in May 1969, the diminutive piston-engined two-seat Bulldog was taken over by Scottish Aviation for export production but was ordered for the RAF in

1972. Entering RAF service from April 1973, the Bulldog replaced the Chipmunk as the standard *ab initio* trainer for embryo pilots prior to jet instructional machines. Fully aerobatic, with ample modern instrumentation, the aircraft provides a near-ideal introduction to Service flying. By the close of 1975 Bulldogs were the full equipment of all the University air squadrons, thereby enabling would-be Service graduates to prepare for their future career.

Squadron Leader H Harvey, MA discusses the Bulldog:

The Scottish Aviation Bulldog is widely used in the Services as a basic trainer, both by the Royal Navy and, more widely, by the Royal Air Force

British Aerospace (Scottish Aviation) Bulldog The Duke of Kent takes a flight with Flight Lieutenant Ian Lawrence while on a visit to the University of Oxford Air Squadron, Abingdon on 27 June 1979. The Bulldog is a two-seater primary trainer and is highly aerobatic.

with the 16 University Air Squadrons. At RAF Abingdon there are two University Air Squadrons, that of London which has 9 aircraft with 8 instructors and about 80 students, and Oxford with 4 aircraft, 4 instructors and 33 students.

We have found the Bulldog ideal for training novice pilots. They are reasonably sturdy and resilient with a good record of serviceability

198

although they did have a few teething troubles initially. With a fuel capacity of 32 gallons the Bulldog has a range of over 300 nautical miles at its cruising speed of 120 knots which affords a wide scope for student cross country flights. In fact I have never known a situation where anyone has been embarrassed for fuel, whereas on the Chipmunk, which the Bulldog replaced, this did sometimes occur. One feature we lack on the aircraft is navigation aids. This can present a challenge to the instructors when flying above total cloud cover.

The students, most of whom have never flown an aircraft before coming to us, attend for flying training once a week during term time. With occasional extra sessions they can reach 35 hours in a year by which time they are ready for their Basic Handling Test. Apart from normal aircraft handling they are by now proficient enough to perform stalling, spinning and the basic aerobatics. One feature of the Bulldog is that it requires positive spin recovery action which, in a training aircraft is, in my view, a very worthwhile facet. It is also cleared for the full spectrum of aerobatics but, because our aircraft engines are not fitted with the inverted oil system, we are not cleared for sustained inverted flight for more than eight seconds.

By the end of their second year our students are competent at instrument flying and cross country navigation, and the few who complete a third year learn formation flying and have a basic grounding on low level navigation. We find that at this stage there is little left in the Bulldog to stretch the student pilot who is now ready for the greater demands of the Jet Provost at Cranwell.

British Aerospace (Hawker Siddeley) Hawk

In a bid to rationalise all pre-operational training within the RAF, the tandem, two-seat, multi-purpose jet trainer Hawk was designed to replace the Gnat, Hunter and Jet Provost in most aspects. With a maximum speed approaching 600 mph, and built-in provision for fitting bombs, guns and missiles, the Hawk offers a package deal for all stages of jet instruction to future squadron crews. The design first entered RAF use in mid-1977 at No. 4 FTS, Valley and at CFS. Its high-placed rear seat for an instructor permits an excellent field of vision, while the all-round performance of the Hawk gives the student pilot unsurpassed grounding in his future trade. Hawks have now also formed the latest equipment of the RAF's premier aerobatic and exhibition formation team, the Red Arrows, exemplifying not only the supreme skill and precision of the team's crews but demonstrating the agility and exacting control responses inherent in the Hawk.

Squadron Leader Brian Hoskins, the leader of the Red Arrows, has a high opinion of the Hawk:

I converted to the Hawk in the summer of 1979,

199

when the Red Arrows were still flying the Gnat, so that I was able to collect the first Hawk from British Aerospace on 15 September 1979. The team started flying the aircraft extensively from October, and it says a lot for the aeroplane that over just one winter period we were able to prepare for our normal Red Arrow displays in it. We began doing our displays again as usual the following April.

The Hawk is undoubtedly a more advanced plane than the Gnat, and it's a very comfortable one to fly. Its major advantages are that it is extremely reliable, and both carries more fuel and has a far more efficient engine than the Gnat. As a result, we can get a much greater flexibility in diversion: we can finish one display and go on much further than we could before. Last year, we did more than 120

British Aerospace (Hawker Siddeley) Hawk A Hawk from 234 Squadron lets loose a salvo of SNEB rockets on the Pembrey Range off the coast of Dyfed. The Hawk is the successor to the Gnat for the Red Arrows but is otherwise used by the RAF solely as a training aircraft.

displays, and the aircraft performed very well indeed. I cannot visualise any limit on the time we shall use the Hawk. I would have thought it will be in service for very many years, and will be flown by the Red Arrows for a long time to come.

The displays we do with the Hawk are essentially the same as we did with the Gnat. But we do need rather more anticipation than we needed with the Gnat; the Hawk has forced us to change our *technique a bit, especially with the throttle. In particular you need to use the air-brakes against power much more than in the Gnat.*

Another feature of the Hawk is that it is an excellent trainer. It is supersonic, you can fly it on long sorties, you can spin the aeroplane, and, of course, it is very easy to handle in aerobatic formation. A real advantage is that, as well as serving as an advanced trainer, you can use it for

weapon training. It's a marvellous turning aeroplane; its wing is very strong and produces plenty of lift; and when you get into the Hawk the good thing is that it feels as if the entire plane really has been designed to help you do your job. Everything is exactly as it should be to make it easy for you to fly. In fact, I would think that the Hawk's only fault as a trainer is that it may be just a little too easy to fly.

SEPECAT Jaguar

The Jaguar ground-attack fighter represents the first of a new breed of European aircraft. Its design conception gives priority to the low-level assault role, with traditional fighter air-to-air combat capability of a high order yet secondary in consideration. An Anglo-French project from the outset, the Jaguar first achieved operational status on joining the *Escadron 1/7 "Provence"* of the French *Armee de l'Air* in June 1973, while the first Jaguar-equipped RAF unit was 54 Squadron at Coltishall, Norfolk in September 1973. In the context of the RAF's equipment Jaguars thereby supersede Phan-

toms in the ground attack role, leaving the latter for solely interception duties. Packed into its deceptively slight fuselage are a host of computerised technological advantages, including a weapon-delivery system flexible enough to tackle virtually any form of target in any sort of circumstance, but especially at low level and at high speed. Such is the precision of the technical ironmongery that the traditional duties of a navigator and a bomb aimer are automatically carried out for the pilot by his black boxes. As Paul Millett, BAC Military Division's chief test pilot has recorded, 'Pilots of the last generation

of jet ground attack aircraft find that the task of flying a high-speed, low-level mission has been revolutionised. Jaguar has been designed and developed with the aim of lifting a large and varied weapons load from a small airfield, taking these weapons through defended territory to a pinpoint target, attacking that target with maximum accuracy and returning safely

SEPECAT Jaguar A Jaguar GR1, operated in the photo-reconnaissance role by 11(AC) Squadron, makes a low pass over NATO vehicles during a sortie from Laarbruch in 1980.

to base. All pilots who have flown the Jaguar to-date have been delighted with its handling characteristics.'

Panavia Tornado

As the RAF's immediate future equipment the Tornado MRCA (Multi-Role Combat Aircraft) is a product of a European consortium, and will herald the beginning of a fresh era in

RAF annals. It will, in slightly different variants, fulfil all the former roles of both overland and, to some extent, over-sea strike aircraft and thereby replace the ageing Vulcan and

Buccaneer for such purposes; while as an ADV (Air Defence Variant) the Tornado will take over from the bulkier Phantom. Capable of transonic speeds at ultra-low altitude, in any weathers, by day or night, the Tornado's supremely sophisticated ECM and other computerised technology will permit it to attack all forms of target with absolute precision while effectively blind. First prototypes commenced test-flying from 1974 in Germany, Britain and Italy, each of these countries being scheduled for eventual Tornado re-equipment in their air services. In the case of the RAF planned total Tornado equipment will eventually represent more than half of the service's future combat strength.

Wing Commander Clive Rustin, one of the first RAF testing pilots for the Tornado, has described the aircraft as:

. . . a compromise between the requirements for low-level high-speed target penetration, economic cruise, lower speed manoeuvrability and short field performance. By using a variable sweep wing, high lift devices, and the advanced RB199 engines, the aircraft goes as far as is reasonably possible towards achieving the best of both worlds. The low-level,

Panavia Tornado The Tornado is a multi-role combat aircraft designed to perform six major roles: close air support and battlefield interdiction; counter-air operations; air superiority; interception; naval attack; reconnaissance.

high-speed ride qualities are most impressive, and by fully sweeping the wings, thus reducing gust response, crew comfort can be increased to levels not previously experienced in this environment.

Squadron Leader Roger Beazley's acquaintanceship with the Tornado dates from its early evaluation trials:

By 1976 the three Governments of Germany, Italy and the UK had conducted a series of 'preview' evaluation flights to test the handling qualities of the aircraft, and in the autumn of that year I flew the aeroplane as part of the preview to assess the operational use of the avionics, with Squadron Leader John Gray as navigator. We flew the aeroplane as realistically as possible as far as military pilots were concerned, attempting lengthy low-level sorties and so on. We were very impressed with the aeroplane's potential. For instance, the low-level high-speed ride qualities are most impressive, and by fully sweeping the wings, and thus reducing gust response, the crew comfort can be increased to levels not previously experienced in this environment. This could be a vital factor in easing the crew tasks when carrying out operational low-level terrain following penetrations.

The optimum cruise speeds at the various wing sweep angles are surprisingly low. However, the

fuel curves are fairly flat, particularly with a 66° wing sweep, and the pilot can therefore elect to fly considerably faster for quite a small penalty in consumption. On most aircraft the use of reheat involves a major increase in the fuel consumption, and this one is no exception, but with the high bypass engines the near-doubled thrust in maximum reheat gives a fair measure of return.

Some people have questioned whether any single aircraft could undertake all the roles that have been assigned to the Tornado. However, although the airframe is almost identical the avionics of the Tornado ADV (Air Defence Variant) and the Tornado bomber are radically different, which does make them two separate aircraft. The one thing that is not always accepted or understood is that even if we had a totally multi-role aeroplane, it would be extremely difficult to have a totally multi-role crew, because of training, and therefore one tends to specialise the squadrons.

The Tornado is sometimes compared with the American F-111 as that also has variable sweep wings. The F-111 is a larger aeroplane, indeed the Tornado seems surprisingly small to people who have never seen it before. However, the Tornado has been built to fly truly low-level high speed missions over Northern Europe at any time in any weather, and it will do this certainly as well as the F-111.

Bibliography

Air Gunner, M Henry, Foulis 1964

Aircraft of the RAF since 1918, O Thetford, Putnam 1976

Beaufighter at War, C Bowyer, Ian Allan 1976

Brief Glory, E C Cheesman, Harborough 1946

The Clouds Remember, O Stewart, Gale and Polden 1936

Dakota, A Pearce, Ian Allan 1972

Desert Air Force at War, C Bowyer and C F Shores, Ian Allan 1981

Farewell to Wings, C Lewis, Temple Press 1964

Flying and Soldiering, R Money, Nicholson and Watson 1936

Flying between the Wars, A Wheeler, Foulis 1972

Hampden Special, C Bowyer, Ian Allan 1976

Hurricane at War, C Bowyer, Ian Allan 1974

Lancaster at War, B Goulding and M Garbett, Ian Allan 1971

Liberator and Fortress, C Vincent, Canada's Wings 1975

Mosquito at War, C Bowyer, Ian Allan 1973

Mustang at War, R Freeman, Ian Allan 1974

No Specific Gravity, B J Hurren, Temple Press 1944

Not Peace but a Sword, P Gibbs, Cassell 1943

Pathfinders, William Anderson, Jarrolds 1946

Pilot's Summer, F Tredrey, Duckworth 1939

The Quick and the Dead, W A Waterton, F Muller 1956

Sailor Malan, O Walker, Cassell 1953

Sopwith Camel – King of Combat, C Bowyer, Glasney Press 1978

Spitfire, C Bowyer, Arms and Armour Press 1980

Sunderland at War, C Bowyer, Ian Allan 1976

Test Pilot, N Duke, Wingate 1953

Test Pilot at War, H A Taylor, Ian Allan 1970

To the Ends of the Air, G E Livock, HMSO 1973

Twice Vertical, M Shaw, Macdonalds 1971

Typhoon and Tempest at War, R Beamont and A Reed, Ian Allan 1974

What Were They Like to Fly?, D H Clarke, Ian Allan

Handling a barrage balloon

Index

Acknowledgements

Many people helped in the creation of this book, but the publishers would especially like to thank David Bland, Richard T Riding and Humphrey Wynn.

The main quotation under each of the following headings appears by permission of the following: De Havilland 4–*Aeroplane Monthly* Vol 2 No 4, © IPC Business Press Ltd 1974; Sopwith Camel–*Farewell to Wings*, © Cecil Lewis 1964; SE5a– © *Cross and Cockade* Vol 4; Supermarine Southampton and Fairey III–G E Livock, *To The Ends of The Air*, Crown copyright 1973; Blackburn Iris–*Aeroplane Monthly* Vol 1 No 8, © IPC Business Press Ltd 1973; Vickers Vincent– *Aeroplane Monthly* Vol 7 No 5, © IPC Business Press Ltd 1979; Fairey Battle–D H Clarke, *What Were They Like To Fly*, © Ian Allan; Lockheed Hudson–*Aeroplane Monthly* Vol 7 No 10, © IPC Business Press Ltd 1979; De Havilland Mosquito, Handley Page Halifax and Lancaster Path Finder –*Pathfinders*, © William Anderson 1946; Avro Lancaster–B Goulding and M Garbett, *Lancaster at War*, © Ian Allan 1971; Short Stirling– *Aeroplane Monthly* Vol 5 Nos 11-12, © IPC Business Press Ltd 1977; *Hawker Tempest*–Pierre Clostermann, *The Big Show*, © Chatto and Windus 1958; Avro Anson–*Test Pilot At War*, © H A Taylor 1970.

A Gloster Meteor